Christian Perspectives on the
Limits of Law

Christian Perspectives on the Limits of Law

Edited by

Paul R. Beaumont

PATERNOSTER PRESS

Copyright © 2002 The Editor and Contributors

First published in 2002 by Paternoster Press

08 07 06 05 04 03 02   7 6 5 4 3 2 1

Paternoster Press
is an imprint of Authentic Media,
P.O. Box 300, Carlisle, Cumbria, CA3 0QS, UK
and
P.O. Box 1047, Waynesboro, GA 30830-2047, USA

Website: www.paternoster-publishing.com

The right of Paul R. Beaumont to be identified as the Author of this Work has been asserted by him in accordance with the Copyright, Designs and Patents Act 1988.

All rights reserved. No part of this publication may be reproduced, stored in a retrieval system, or transmitted in any form or by any means, electronic, mechanical, photocopying, recording or otherwise, without the prior permission of the publisher or a licence permitting restricted copying. In the UK such licences are issued by the Copyright Licensing Agency, 90 Tottenham Court Road, London W1P 9HE.

British Library Cataloguing in Publication Data
A catalogue record for this book is available from the British Library

ISBN 1-84227-156-3
Unless otherwise stated, Scripture quotations are taken from the
HOLY BIBLE, NEW INTERNATIONAL VERSION
Copyright © 1973, 1978, 1984 by the International Bible Society.
Used by permission of Hodder and Stoughton Limited. All rights reserved.
'NIV' is a registered trademark of the International Bible Society
UK trademark number 1448790

Cover Design by FourNineZero
Typeset by WestKey Ltd, Falmouth, Cornwall
Printed in Great Britain by Bell & Bain Ltd, Glasgow

Contents

Contributors   vii

Introduction by Paul Beaumont   1

1. Liberal Constitutionalism and Christian Political Thought
Julian Rivers

    I. Introduction   11
    II. Augustine (354–430)   13
    III. William of Ockham (c.1285–c.1347)   17
    IV. Roger Williams (c.1599–1683)   21
    V. Abraham Kuyper (1837–1920)   24
    VI. Liberal Foundations   26
    VII. Liberal Ideals   29
    VIII. Liberal Principles   32
    IX. Conclusions   33

2. The Legal Framework for Religion in Schools in England and Wales: Enforcement or Enablement?
David Harte

    I. Introduction   35
    II. The Legal Place of Religion in English and Welsh Schools Today   36
    III. Enforcement and Enablement as Two Faces to Law   40
    IV. The Utility of the Distinction Between Law as Enforcement and Law as Enablement   44
    V. The Justification for Compulsory Education of Children Generally and for Including Any Specific Compulsory Elements in the Syllabus   47
    VI. Religious Education   51
    VII. The Place of Christianity Within Statutory Religious Education   55
    VIII. Worship   59
    IX. The Church and the Place of Denominational Schools   65
    X. Conclusion   68

3. The Contracting Society: A Misplaced Faith
Ewan McKendrick

    I. Introduction   71
    II. Two Distinctions   72
    III. Is There Such a Thing as a Distinctively Christian Law of Contract?   73

    IV. We Are Not Omniscient 77
    V. Our Pursuit of Self-interest 84
    VI. The Lack of Trust 87
    VII. Conclusion 88

4. **Between a Rock and a Hard Place: Law's Dilemma over Trustees' Ethical Investment**
   Alison Dunn

    I. Introduction 92
    II. Trustee Powers of Investment in English Law 96
    III. Trustee Powers of Investment in Scots Law 103
    IV. Trustee Powers of Investment in United States Law 104
    V. Options 106
    VI. Finding God in the FTSE 100 108
    VII. The Way Forward 111
    VIII. Conclusion 116

5. **Can the Law Ensure Proper Stewardship of Land?**
   Thomas Glyn Watkin

    I. Introduction 119
    II. Differing Views of Ownership 120
    III. Ownership in Past Ages 125
    IV. Modern Restrictions on Ownership 132
    V. What are the Limits of the Law in this Regard? 135
    VI. Christian Stewardship of the Land 137
    VII. How Can Stewardship be Ensured? 142
    VIII. Conclusion 148

Contributors

Paul Beaumont, Professor of Law, University of Aberdeen
Alison Dunn, Lecturer in Law, Newcastle University
David Harte, Senior Lecturer in Law, Newcastle University
Ewan McKendrick, Professor of Law, Oxford University
Julian Rivers, Lecturer in Law, University of Bristol
Thomas Glyn Watkin, Professor of Law, Cardiff University

Introduction

Paul Beaumont

This book grew out of the Fourth Lawyers' Christian Fellowship (LCF) Academic Conference at London Bible College on 10 September 1999 and is in turn the fourth book in the Christian Perspectives on Law Series published by Paternoster,[1] the first three books having grown out of the first three conferences. The chapters in this book are diverse in their subject matter, encompassing political and legal theory, education law, contract and commercial law, equity and trusts, and property and environmental law: there is something for everyone. The theme is discernible from the title of the book: in the areas of law examined the authors perceive that there are limits as to what the law can achieve, and that these perceptions are rooted in the authors' Christian worldview.

Fittingly, the most theoretical chapter comes first. Julian Rivers explores Christian thought on the role of the State through the lens of four Christian thinkers: Augustine, William of Ockham, Roger Williams and Abraham Kuyper. He argues that there is a strong strand in Christian thinking which is consistent with liberalism. The State must not compel people to become Christians, but it must permit people the freedom to live their lives in accordance with Christian principles within the visible church. However, a form of liberalism that emphasises the two spheres of life as being the State and the individual, but which neglects or fails to accommodate the sphere of life of the community or church, is not always able to achieve that objective. Rivers asks us to consider espousing a more nuanced form of liberalism that has a place for the church, rather than rejecting liberalism.

A further example of an attempt to fit Christian perspectives into a liberal framework is found in David Harte's advocacy of seeing the requirement to have acts of religious worship and religious education in

---

[1] Paul Beaumont (ed.), *Christian Perspectives on Law Reform* (Carlisle, Paternoster, 1998); Paul Beaumont (ed.), *Christian Perspectives on Human Rights and Legal Philosophy* (Carlisle, Paternoster, 1998); Paul Beaumont and Keith Wotherspoon (eds.), *Christian Perspectives on Law and Relationism* (Carlisle, Paternoster, 2000). The books can be obtained from the Lawyers' Christian Fellowship or via the Web on www.lawcf.org.

schools in England and Wales as 'enabling' children to learn about and practise religion rather than enforcing them to do so. He makes a good case for viewing law as an enabler and for this being a way of creating allies for Christian thinking so that it can become part of the law of the land in a country where most people are not participants in a religious group. Clearly there is a good case for saying that all children should be enabled to learn something about the major religious beliefs in the world and, in particular, to know about Christianity, which has played such a major part in the history of the Western world. The freedom of parents who object to such religious education – either because it may water down the beliefs they are trying to teach their children or because it may give their children religious beliefs that they do not want them to have – to withdraw their children from it may be sufficient to permit us to see the present law as enabling rather than enforcing.

It could be argued, however, that there are other ways of enabling children to learn about religion. First, parents could be encouraged to opt their children in to religious education rather in the way that parents have to do if they want their children to have lessons to be able to learn a musical instrument. At least at the primary school level this seems to give too little weight to the importance of religious knowledge for an understanding of history and ideas. At primary school children learn about music even if their opportunities for putting it into practice by playing an instrument are limited to those whose parents will opt them in to (pay for) the lessons. Another path to enablement is for the State to pay for confessional schools so that the whole ethos of the school can be built around the worldview propagated by the religious group running the school. So there can be, for example, Christian, Jewish and Muslim schools, in addition to secular schools, in all communities where there are sufficient parents willing to send their children to such schools to justify their existence. This permits children not only to hear about religion as an academic subject in its own right, but to see how the religion is worked out in a community and to practise their religious beliefs to the full.

The problem with this scenario from a liberal viewpoint is that it may not enable children to get a different worldview from that of their parents and to make an independent choice as to which, if any, religious faith they wish to adopt. This liberal viewpoint may indeed be a Christian viewpoint because Christians believe that people should not be compelled to accept Christ, but rather choose to do so. Although Christian parents will desire that their children come to faith in Christ they will not all think it appropriate that their children should receive all their education in a Christian environment.[2] Many will feel that their children must be able to make a genuine choice to follow Christ and that if they do so they must be

---

[2] See Rex Ahdar, 'Parental Religious Upbringing in a Children's Rights Era', in Beaumont and Wotherspoon, *Christian Perspectives on Law and Relationism*, 189–235.

enabled to prepare for living in a society where most people have chosen not to follow Christ. The enablement may be best provided by a combination of Christian education in the home and in a church, and general education in non-confessional schools. The children who have not yet come to faith in Christ will see that there are alternatives to the faith of their parents and be able to make an informed choice, while those children who have accepted Christ will be able to be salt and light in the largely secular local school. For those Christian parents who think it best to have the whole of their children's education from a Christian perspective they should at least have the option of providing appropriate home schooling or placing their children in a privately funded confessional school. Is it really appropriate for society to fund an education system divided on confessional lines? Has this been a positive experience in Northern Ireland?

Christians will disagree on the best solution in this context and what constitutes the appropriate 'enabling' solution. I would like to see children of different faiths and none kept together in the same schools. In order for this to work it may be necessary to leave formal teaching about religious belief entirely out of the State school system other than permitting voluntary groups to meet at lunchtimes and after school (e.g. Scripture Union meetings). It would be sad if children from non-faith homes gained no understanding of the faith of others in the classroom. However, it is also sad if children gain an erroneous understanding of the faith of others by half-baked and watered-down presentations of religious belief in the classroom. Do we want people to know that Jesus was a good man who taught us to love other people? Or to know that Jesus is the Son of God who is the only way to God through belief in his death and resurrection providing the means for our moral failures to be forgiven? The latter may be best attained through extra-curricular means rather than via the curriculum, which is likely to be driven down to the lowest common denominator of what Christians believe about their own faith.

Alternatively, the best path to enablement may be a robust form of religious education that shows the full extent of the beliefs of people adhering to the major world religions, and that these beliefs conflict. This may enable children to learn that we have to respect the views of others even when we disagree with them, that religious faith or none is an issue that divides people and goes to the very heart of their approach to life, and that these divisions cannot be wished away by syncretism. Either religious education needs to be removed from schools or it needs to be of a high quality with teachers avoiding scepticism about religion, avoiding teaching only the non-contentious shared values of different religions and avoiding indoctrination while giving a full and fair view of the claims of the major religions.

It is difficult to reconcile Julian Rivers' advocacy of the visible church being voluntary with David Harte's advocacy of acts of worship in non-confessional schools. To achieve reconciliation the act of worship has to cease to be worship of the true and living God or it has to become genuinely voluntary by requiring students to opt in to it rather than their parents opting them out of it. David Harte seems to be willing to go down the route of the former by restricting these acts of worship to readings and songs. I would prefer to remove worship from State schools or alternatively to allow school chaplains and other people committed to a particular faith to be given space within the school to offer on a voluntary basis worship services for students. So students could choose according to their own beliefs whether they wish to attend a Christian or Jewish or Muslim act of worship. Admittedly, the voluntary nature of the visible church is under strain whenever we are dealing with children, because their parents often require them to attend a church. The age at which children should be permitted to decline to go to church or to decline to attend worship in schools that their parents want them to attend is a matter for debate. If worship is to be provided in a State school on a voluntary basis, then perhaps up to the age of twelve it should be for the parents to choose to opt their child in or not, and from the age of thirteen onwards for the child to choose to opt in or not. Such a rule for school could only be a guideline in relation to the question of attendance at church.

There is a danger that removing worship from State schools will remove a possible experience of the wonder of God from children who do not have the opportunity to worship God in their homes or in a faith community. This danger has to be weighed against the risk that such children will regard the worship experiences in school as alien, uninspired, hypocritical or dead, and will assume that all worship is like that. An enabling framework would seem to be worship on an opt-in basis or, better still, leaving it to voluntary groups to provide worship as an extra-curricular activity in schools. For children from non-faith homes it is probably better that they be exposed to no worship than be exposed to poor worship, or confused interfaith worship, or even vibrant, real worship, if they have in effect been compelled into it because their parents have not opted them out of it. For a child from a faith home it is not difficult for their parents to provide sufficient opportunities for them to worship God in their homes and in their churches, synagogues, mosques, and so on.

Ewan McKendrick's chapter is sensitive to the need to avoid 'imposing' by way of law Christian values on a pluralist society. He lucidly demonstrates that few Christian values underpin the law of contract, and that the values which do exist (e.g. fidelity of parties to their obligations) should not be regarded as absolute. A thoughtful use of examples from real and imagined cases enables McKendrick to show that the cognitive limitations which apply to humans, the inherent tendency in all humans to pursue self-interest, and the difficulty that people have to put their trust in others all point to a non-absolute approach to holding people to their promises. He also points out that many of the difficult policy questions in the law of contract – one can include many other areas of law too, like private international law – turn on striking the balance between legal certainty and trying to do justice in the individual case. McKendrick argues that Christian principles do not give us an insight as to where this balance should be struck.

It seems to me, however, that his own arguments show that Christian principles probably tilt the balance in favour of legal certainty rather than justice in the individual case. The reason for this is that emphasising certainty leads in most cases to upholding the underlying principle that people should be held to their bargain (or respect for party autonomy). A neglect of certainty leads to more litigation because it will not be clear on what basis justice will be done in the individual case. It would seem to be a Christian principle to try to minimise the number of contractual disputes that are resolved in court because it is wasteful of resources and can be damaging to relationships.[3] Thus the legislature and judges should be very cautious before introducing any exceptions to the principle of party autonomy. When such exceptions are introduced the legislature should define them as carefully as possible and the judges should be careful to enable future cases to be settled out of court by providing as clear guidance as possible in decided cases as to when the exception to parties being held to their bargain is to apply.

This analysis can be applied to whether there should be a duty of disclosure (transparency) in contractual relationships. Is it not too uncertain a requirement to impose on parties a duty to disclose anything that might be relevant to the bargain that the parties are about to enter into? If the law wishes to maintain certainty in this area it should state precisely the kind of information that a party has a duty to disclose. It may, for example, be reasonable to impose an obligation on a buyer in an e-commerce contract to disclose where they are resident so that the seller can decide whether or not to deliver goods on-line and become exposed to the jurisdiction of the courts of the buyer's residence. Such a duty of disclosure is simply designed to avoid a buyer pretending to be in a particular country solely to enable them to get on-line delivery that the seller would not make if they knew where the buyer was resident.

McKendrick is rightly sceptical about confusing contract law and trusts and argues that multinational companies should be free to exclude fiduciary duties from the scope of a joint venture. This is part of the respect owed to party autonomy, especially in the sphere of business-to-business contracts. Interestingly, McKendrick doubts the value of transporting the contractual relationship, based on bargaining between parties rather than mutual trust, into the health service, family law and the relationship between parents and schools. Each of these areas

---

[3] For a relational approach to contracts see Stephen Copp, 'Developing a Relationally Based Law of Contract: A Question of Good Faith?' in Beaumont and Wotherspoon, *Christian Perspectives on Law and Relationism*, 53–92.

needs careful and separate attention. In relation to the school context it is relevant to ask how schools are to engage with parents unless they at least get them to sign sheets releasing their children to attend school trips, or to explain their absence, or to verify that they have done their homework. It does not seem unreasonable to go a step further and ask parents to sign up to certain minimum obligations that they agree to keep in relation to the school, and for the school to agree to certain minimum requirements that it will uphold.

It is difficult to see any Christian principles that are offended by a written agreement between parents and a school of the kind outlined by McKendrick. He is of course right that the only way to transform society radically for the better is by individuals having their relationship with God restored, leading to those individuals improving their relationships with others. However, more modest social reforms can help to make human relationships better. Whereas a family relationship should be built on trust and love rather than contract, it is not so clear that a relationship between a school and parents cannot be initiated by contract, even though in some cases it may blossom into one of mutual trust. The contract may help to foster a relationship that might not otherwise exist, because the school may not value parental contributions, or the parent may not want to interact with the school. Admittedly, a minimalist approach to the contract will lead to lip service being paid to the relationship between the school and the parents, but there is no reason to assume that the contract will not be seen as a foundation – a minimum floor – upon which a meaningful relationship can be built, which goes well beyond its terms.

Alison Dunn highlights the dilemma facing the Christian law reformer in analysing the appropriate balance between protecting the financial interests of trust beneficiaries (which point towards a duty of care on trustees to seek to maximise the financial return for beneficiaries), and enabling trustees to make investment decisions consistent with Christian ethical standards (which may mean avoiding the most lucrative investments if the companies being invested in behave unethically: e.g. by using child labour, utilising environmental resources in an unsustainable way, or selling tobacco or pornography). The problem can be reduced by persuading settlors to establish ethical investment criteria in the trust deed that trustees must follow. In the absence of clarity in the trust deed, legislation could be introduced to give trustees a positive duty to invest ethically or at least to be free to avoid unethical investments even where this may reduce the financial return for the beneficiaries.

Legislative reform is not rejected by Dunn, but she is conscious of the difficulty of defining what constitutes an ethical investment and what constitutes an unethical investment. It seems possible to have investments that are not unethical but which have no positive aspiration to being regarded as ethical. Logically, however, an investment is either unethical or ethical and no grey zone exists. What people might mean when they refer to ethical investments is an investment in a company which is positively promoting a morally 'good' value (e.g. selling only organic products), and when they refer to unethical investments they mean companies promoting a morally 'bad' value (e.g. selling products made by children who are paid almost nothing). In fact, most companies avoid promoting the morally bad, but do not exclusively promote the morally good. So should the legislature give trustees a legal obligation to invest some or all of trust funds in companies that are morally good, and could a pluralist society agree on what the morally good is in this context? Alternatively, should the legislature attempt to define the sorts of actions that make a company morally bad, and therefore prevent trustees from investing in such companies?

It seems to me beyond the limits of the law, from a Christian perspective, for the legislature to enter into moral rather than legal judgements. If a company's behaviour is sufficiently unethical that it is illegal (e.g. using child slave labour abroad, or not paying the minimum wage in the UK and observing the rules about limited hours of work for children) then the company should be prosecuted and prevented from continuing the illegal behaviour. If individuals are free to invest in any company, then trustees should be free to do so, unless the settlor decides to the contrary. This means that, absent the settlor determining the matter, trustees should be free to choose to invest in companies that purport to be exclusively engaged in the morally good. The worry is that trustees might damage the financial interests of the beneficiaries too much if they invest exclusively or too heavily in such companies. Dunn suggests that the courts may be able to provide the protection by carefully balancing the needs of the beneficiaries with the sensitive ethical consciences of the trustees. Trustees should not be compelled to make investment decisions with wealth maximisation for the beneficiaries as the overriding objective; rather, they should be required to make prudent investment decisions that will secure at least a reasonable return for the beneficiaries without being compelled to invest in a company that promotes something the trustees regard as morally bad (e.g. pornography).

Giving trustees the freedom to invest as they see fit is an attractive solution. The best remedy against trustees choosing to invest in companies promoting morally bad values is adverse publicity and public pressure. The best way to police the occasional overzealous investment in companies that promote the morally good, but are unlikely to deliver a reasonable financial return for the beneficiaries, is to give the beneficiaries redress against the trustees in the courts for a clear breach of their duty of care. Trust law cannot become the guardian of morality by prescribing the types of investment that are morally acceptable and those that are not.

Christians will want to give freedom to trustees to pursue investments in companies that promote, or act consistently with, Christian (not necessarily the same as ethical) values, but not at the expense of a reasonable return for the beneficiaries. Christians, in the absence of the instructions of the settlor to do so, will not want to compel trustees to make such investments. The Christian belief in the liberty of the individual to make good or bad moral choices should extend to trustees, provided they act in accordance with the trust deed and their duty of care to the beneficiaries. The limits on the trustees' freedom to make investment decisions imposed by the duty of care cannot be reduced to a simple legal formula conducive to legal certainty, but it should not be so open ended as to encourage litigation. It is possible to suggest that trustees would be in breach of their duty of care when their investment decisions create a risk of a considerably below-optimum financial return for the beneficiaries, or where the nature of the investments is clearly inconsistent with the purpose of the body the trust is set up to support (e.g. where the trust is set up to manage the property of a church, and the investment is in a company selling pornography).

Thomas Watkin moves us from the stewardship of property by trustees to the stewardship of land by those who own it. Building on the work of Alan Rodger he shows that ownership of property was not an absolute concept in Roman Law and throughout most of legal history. The modern development in private law of a more absolute concept of ownership has been counterbalanced by the growth in public law in the twentieth century controlling the use of land for the public good through planning and environmental law. Watkins carefully considers different theological views on humankind's relationship with creation after the fall and links them to the modern notion of sustainable development. His Christian perspective leads him to advocate that Christians should regard the land as part of God's gift of creation and that we have a responsibility to be good stewards of the land. The biblical approach to stewardship is to make good use of the land. Watkins is bullish about trusting God for new energy resources and therefore making appropriate use of non-renewable energy resources. The Christian does not see creation as a static resource to be conserved, but rather as a dynamic work of God's creation that includes the ability of humans to develop new means of generating energy. Paradoxically, Watkins warns against the dangers of profit maximisation and too much competition leading to the overexploitation by corporations and individuals of land and the resources contained in it. Watkins does not explore what sorts of limits the law can and should place on the use of land by owners – that would be the work of a book. He rightly points out that even the best legal regime regulating the use of land is no substitute for a work of 'grace' in the hearts of landowners, giving them an insight into God's will for the use of their land.

It is encouraging to note that in recent times there has been an upsurge in literature examining the relationship between law and religion, in particular between law and Christianity, and that a reasonable amount of it is written from a Christian perspective. The four books in the Christian Perspectives series published by Paternoster were noted at the beginning of this introduction. The LCF Academic Conferences that led to these books continue, and there may in the future be more books in the series. There is a short book, *Law and Christian Ethics*, containing the texts of a series of lectures given under the auspices of the Church of Scotland Board of Social Responsibility and the Centre for Theology and Public Issues, University of Edinburgh.[4] One of the previous contributors to the Christian Perspectives series, Rex Ahdar, has edited an interesting collection of essays entitled *Law and Religion*.[5] Finally, a major colloquium on Law and Religion at University College, London, in the summer of 2000 has resulted in the volume on *Law and Religion: Current Legal Issues 2001*.[6] This contains many useful articles, and includes a contribution by me that attempts to draw together some of the ideas from the Christian Perspectives series in a chapter entitled 'Christian Perspectives on the Law: What Makes them Distinctive?'

I trust that this book and the other literature just noted will enable Christian law students, academics, practitioners and judges to think through their attitude to what the law should be from a Christian perspective. On many issues the books reveal a range of positions that Christians can hold while being faithful to biblical teaching. Christians will often not be able to speak with one voice, but at least they should be able to understand the range of opinions and be able to engage in an informed debate within the Christian community, as well as engaging in debate beyond the Christian community in the arena of legal policy-making. I also hope that lawyers and policy-makers who are not practising Christians will read this book and the others mentioned, to enable them to understand better the perspectives of those who have a

[4] Edinburgh, Saint Andrew Press, 2001. Of particular interest are Lord Mackay of Clashfern, 'The Law and Christian Ethics: Yesterday and Today', at 1–13; Stephen Copp, 'The Law and Christian Ethics in Business', at 36–75; Alastair V. Campbell, 'Medical Dilemmas and the Law', at 76–87; and Paul Beaumont, 'Christianity and Law Reform: A Living Tradition', at 88–104.

[5] Aldershot, Dartmouth, 2000. This is an international and erudite collection. Of particular interest is the insight into US law provided by Michael W. McConnell, 'Neutrality, Separation and Accommodation: Tensions in American First Amendment Doctrine', at 63–79; and Marie A. Failinger, 'Wondering after Babel: Power, Freedom and Ideology in US Supreme Court Interpretations of the Religion Clauses', at 81–109; the introductory chapter by Rex Ahdar, 'The Inevitability of Law and Religion: An Introduction', at 1–15; the foreword by Lord Mackay of Clashfern; Malcolm Evans, 'The United Nations and Freedom of Religion: The Work of the Human Rights Committee', at 35–61; Julian Rivers, 'From Toleration to Pluralism: Religious Liberty and Religious Establishment under the United Kingdom's Human Rights Act', at 133–161; and Reid Mortensen, 'Art, Expression and the Offended Believer', at 181–197.

[6] Vol. 4, Richard O'Dair and Andrew Lewis (eds.) (Oxford, Oxford University Press, 2001).

Christian worldview. It would be helpful if the books were to be ordered for public and university libraries so that the Christian and non-Christian constituencies of lawyers and policy-makers will have easy access to them. Perhaps this increased understanding will lead to wiser, more sensitive law-making.

Finally, I wish to thank the contributors to this volume for their patience with the very long time taken to turn their papers into a publication, Tony Graham for his continued help and forbearance at Paternoster, LCF for supporting this venture (all authors' royalties from the book go to LCF), London Bible College for providing an excellent venue for the LCF Academic Conference in 1999 at which earlier versions of these papers were given, the participants at that conference for their comments, the referees (two per chapter) who gave helpful comments on each of the draft chapters, and Maureen Mercer for doing the secretarial work for the book and the conference.

1

Liberal Constitutionalism and Christian Political Thought

Julian Rivers[1]

I. Introduction

The idea that law is limited lies at the heart of the Christian gospel: we are saved by grace, not by law, and if adherence to the moral law is powerless to restore us to relationship with God, still less is any possible civil law.[2] Furthermore, Christians are going to be quick to insist that inherent sinfulness makes it hard for people to obey law. However, there is a different sense in which law might be limited: the idea that civil government might, as a matter of moral principle, have limited functions, that there might be a sphere of social life out of bounds for the law.[3] It is a hallmark of liberal theories of justice that they take seriously the task of finding a coherent basis on which to set limits to law. Liberalism is, of course, a broad tradition of political thought, embracing the libertarianism of Locke and Nozick and the egalitarianism of Rawls, the optimism of the French *philosophes*, and the realism of Adam Smith, but the tradition has certain common themes. In spite of all the disagreements within liberalism about human nature and the distribution of property, there is at least broad agreement on the value of liberal constitutionalism. Stephen Macedo summarises the key elements of liberal constitutionalism in this way: 'Liberal politics stands, first and foremost, for individual freedom and rights, the rule of law, limited and accountable government.'[4]

---

[1] I am grateful to John Coffey and Robert Song for their perceptive comments on an earlier draft.

[2] Rom. 3:21: 'But now a righteousness from God, apart from law, has been made known ...'

[3] To say that government might have limited functions is not to say that law is limited in the same way; Hayek is well known for arguing that there is a law of liberty spontaneous to all societies, and which is to be distinguished from legislation: F.A. Hayek, *Law, Legislation and Liberty* (London, Routledge, 1998), esp. Vol. 1 (*Rules and Order*). I am concerned here primarily with law as an instrument of government power and want to leave open the question of the role of law within non-state spheres.

[4] Stephen Macedo, *Liberal Virtues* (Oxford, Clarendon Press, 1991), 2.

Christians often respond to the limits that liberals typically set to the law with mixed feelings. The freedom to meet and worship God as one sees fit is valued, but what about freedom to look at pornography, and abort one's child? The equality of all human beings is affirmed, but what about the interchangeability of gender roles in the family, or non-discrimination on the grounds of sexual orientation? Private property is generally considered a just institution, but what about a society in which the managing director earns more than a hundred times the wage of the office cleaner? Should the possession of cannabis be criminally proscribed? Should taxation be proportional or progressive?

It is not the purpose of this chapter to give an answer to these problems, although some answers are implied by its conclusions. Rather, its purpose is to consider some of the connections between the liberal concern to limit government (liberal constitutionalism) and the Christian tradition of political thought. It is not suggested that the late medieval Franciscan thinkers, or the radical Puritans, were closet liberals in any recognisably modern sense; they were not. Nor is it suggested that the history of Christian political theory represents an unbroken line of gradual intellectual development of which liberalism is the crowning glory; it does not. There is no simple relationship between Christianity and liberal political theory.[5] In an earlier volume in this series, Ian Leigh has rightly pointed out the divergences between Christianity and modern liberal conceptions of religion and religious liberty.[6] Yet to treat these as the expression of a fundamental opposition between two monolithic entities, 'Liberalism' and 'Christianity' is too easy. Some of Leigh's conclusions converge with mainstream liberal thought, and this should not surprise us, for there is a strand of thinking within the Christian political tradition that is essentially liberal in its principled concern to limit the role of government and secular law. By considering the work of four major Christian political theorists, this chapter will consider the foundations of a Christian political liberalism, and compare them with the justifications commonly offered by liberals for their principles of justice. The tentative conclusion will be that although the liberalism[7] of Christians is likely to be more limited than that of most secular liberals, it will also be more robust.

[5] Considerations of the relationship between Christianity and liberalism are rare. A most valuable exception is Robert Song, *Christianity and Liberal Society* (Oxford, Clarendon Press, 1997).

6 Ian Leigh, 'Towards a Christian Approach to Religious Liberty', in Paul Beaumont (ed.), *Christian Perspectives on Human Rights and Legal Philosophy* (Carlisle, Paternoster, 1998). I am sympathetic with much of Leigh's critique of 'Liberalism', but would rather see the issues couched in terms of a debate within liberalism as to its best conception.

7 It should be clear that by 'liberalism' in this chapter I am referring only to political liberalism, not theological liberalism.

II. Augustine (354–430)

In Book 19 of the *City of God*, Augustine sets a problem for Christian political thought. Adopting first of all Cicero's definition of a state as a 'multitude united in association by a common sense of justice and a community of interest', he points out that since justice requires giving each person their due, which in turn requires that we love God as well as our neighbour, it would seem that justice, and hence a state, can only exist among Christians.[8] So Augustine considers a different definition: 'a nation is the association of a multitude of rational beings united by a common agreement on the objects of their love'.[9] The better the objects, the better the nation; and conversely.

What are we to make of this argument? At no point did Augustine set out to develop a political theory, and even allowing for the development of his thought over time, it is not easy to reconstruct a coherent theory of justice out of his writing. Among commentators, there are three broad interpretations. The medieval theorists read Augustine as a perfectionist within the classical tradition, and as a theocrat. Church and government are part of a natural order leading to God. The church, being an association of Christians, is a more just society than the state, and thus has a greater claim to political allegiance. Governments are the servants of the church in carrying out secular tasks, which belong by right to the church but are delegated to the state for convenience's sake.[10] At the other extreme, it is possible to read Augustine in the opposite sense as the last of the early Christians: a realist and a pietist. Earthly society always was, and always will be, composed of those who fail to worship God. There can be no justice in the political order, which reflects the realm of sin and Satan. Our only hope is in the City of God to be revealed from heaven at the end of time.[11]

Although radically opposed, these two interpretations have one thing in common: they both assume that Augustine did not develop a conception of justice that required anything less than full-blooded Christian commitment. Certainly, there is no systematic exposition of this problem, or the competing interpretations would not have arisen, but

---

[8] *City of God*, tr. Henry Bettenson (Harmondsworth, Penguin Classics, 1984), Bk. 19, ch. 23.
[9] *Ibid.* ch. 24.
[10] In modern times, this interpretation is followed by George H. Sabine, *A History of Political Theory*, (London, G.G. Harrap, 3rd ed. 1963), 180–197; Charles McIlwain, *The Growth of Political Thought in the West* (New York, Cooper Square, 1968), 154 ff.
[11] Christopher Kirwan, *Augustine* (London, Routledge, 1989), ch. 11. John Rist's nuanced account in *Augustine: Ancient Thought Baptised* (Cambridge, Cambridge University Press, 1994), ch. 6, also tends in this direction.

both fail to account for some important features of his work. Augustine's thought, as is well known, is dominated by a massive dualism between the earthly city and the City of God. A number of commentators from Carlyle[12] and Figgis[13] onwards have argued that the medieval interpreters were fundamentally mistaken in assimilating those two concepts to the state and the church, making the former subject to the latter. For Augustine, both of these societies ('cities') are mystical entities only to be disentangled at the day of judgement. The earthly city is the mass of humanity without God, and the City of God is redeemed humanity under God. There is no equivalent parallelism between church and state, because while the church seeks to symbolise, or point towards, the City of God, the state is simply an organised cross-section of human society, Christian and non-Christian.

Attention to Augustine's language confirms that he saw a limited good in organised society, and an emphasis on this limited good is the hallmark of 'liberal' interpretations of Augustine. What he says is that without the worship of Christ there is no *true* justice. In Book 19, chapter 26, of the *City of God* he argues that the 'peace of Babylon' is valuable because it can be put to good use. Peace and good order in society enable the people of God to live godly lives. This is not true peace – peace with God – but it is a valuable peace nonetheless. Likewise, in discussing the virtues of rulers in Book 5, Augustine distinguishes between the (relatively good) ambition for glory and the (evil) ambition for domination. The Romans were virtuous according to the standards of the earthly city, and, although it was not true virtue, it was a sort of virtue. In his image of the 'conscientious judge' he underestimates neither the gruesome nature of the task in which he is involved, nor its moral necessity.[14] Thus Augustine accepts that there is a limited conception of justice that applies for all people, and a limited set of virtues short of Christian perfection that all governments should display. In this way he legitimises governmental functions of the maintenance of defence and public order, and the role of law in maintaining property relations, protecting individuals from harm and enforcing contracts.[15]

---

[12] R.W. and A.J. Carlyle, *A History of Political Theory in the West* (Edinburgh, Blackwood, 1903–36), Vol. 1, 164–270.

[13] J.N. Figgis, *The Political Aspects of St. Augustine's City of God* (London, Longmans, Green, 1921); Herbert A. Deane, *The Political and Social Ideas of St. Augustine* (New York, Columbia University Press, 1963); R.A. Markus, *Saeculum: History and Society in the Theology of St. Augustine* (Cambridge, Cambridge University Press, 1970), ch. 4.

[14] Markus, *Saeculum*, 99–100.

[15] Augustine appears to have acknowledged the necessity for some measure of state-supported cultural coherence as well: see Markus, *Saeculum*, 96.

These three approaches to the interpretation of Augustine's political thought are exemplified in the attitude of commentators to his famous sentiment that states without justice are nothing other than large bands of robbers.[16] For those who see Augustine as one with classical and medieval perfectionism, the comment serves to press home the necessity of (Christian) justice if the state is to avoid political illegitimacy.[17] For the realist, Augustine is pointing out that there is no moral difference between governments and robbers, between an Alexander the Great and a pirate.[18] And for the liberal, Augustine is highlighting the minimum of authority, order and justice that will obtain in any organised society, even in a society of robbers.[19]

In fact, Augustine's political thought is marked by two contrapuntal, and at first sight contradictory, lines of development. On one hand, his work is marked by an increasing pessimism about the role of the state.[20] Where initially he was inclined to a classical view of the state, in which government fulfils a valuable role in God's natural order by assisting in the formation of perfect society, increasingly he argued that the most the state could do is to restrain sin and disorder, creating the opportunity for the development of Christian virtue, but without contributing to it positively.[21] This development can also be seen in his concept of law. Initially, he suggested that human law inconsistent with divine law was invalid, but later on he states that the eternal law is simply a model that the good legislator will wish to follow. In general, the Christian should submit to authority in the same way as he submits to any other painful necessity of this sin-ridden world, such as illness. Thus there is in this respect a move from perfectionism to realism.

On the other hand, Augustine increasingly accepted the legitimacy of state coercion in matters of faith.[22] In discussing the virtues of rulers he stated that an emperor is truly happy if he 'puts his power at the service of God's majesty to extend his worship far and wide'.[23] Yet the issue was still how that imperial power might legitimately be exercised. He never appeared to have any problem with the Christian emperors outlawing pagan sacrifices. Yet he was at first opposed to imperial involvement in

---

[16] *City of God*, Bk. 4, ch. 4.
[17] McIlwain, *Growth of Political Thought*, 155–160. The Carlyles read this passage in the same way, thus failing to see anything other than a contradiction with the basic thrust of his work (Carlyles, *History of Political Theory*, 167–168).
[18] Kirwan, *Augustine*, 219–220; Rist, *Augustine*, 219.
[19] Deane, *Political and Social Ideas*, 126–128.
[20] Markus, *Saeculum*, gives a good account of this development.
[21] Note that this later position is not necessarily incompatible with a 'maximalist' state engaging in the redistribution of wealth. I am grateful to Robert Song for pointing this out to me.
[22] See Deane, *Political and Social Ideas*, ch. 6; and Kirwan, *Augustine*, 209–218.
[23] *City of God*, Bk. 5, ch. 24.

church affairs. At least until AD 398 he maintained the position 'that no one should be coerced into the unity of Christ, that we must act only by words, fight only by arguments, and prevail by force of reason, lest we should have those whom we knew as avowed heretics feigning themselves to be Catholics'.[24]

Thus there was to be freedom of thought for both Manichaeans and Donatists. What changed him was his experience of the Donatist schism in North Africa.[25] Augustine increasingly accepted that the church needed protection from acts of violence committed by members of the Donatist sect, by threatening the leading Donatist clergy with fines, consfiscation of property and office, and exile. Then, from about AD 408 onwards, we find Augustine openly admitting that he had changed his mind. The church had a duty to ask government to punish schismatics and heretics as such, and this not only against the Donatists, who formented public disorder and had appealed for imperial intervention in the first instance, but also later against the Pelagians. The purpose of force in matters of faith was still persuasion, not punishment, as was demonstrated by his opposition to capital punishment, and his general pleas for leniency. But external pressure seemed to work, prompting a change of heart in the matter of religious persecution, a change of heart that seems, at first, to reflect a move from realism towards a perfectionist view of the state.

Are these two lines of development coherent? The clue lies in one of the key texts Augustine used to legitimise the use of force against heretics: *compelle* (or *coge*) *intrare*, 'force them to come in', from the parable of the Great Banquet in Luke 14:15–24, which he used as a figure of the church.[26] Augustine knew it was impossible to change people's minds – only God could do that – but one could create the social conditions under which people were protected from going astray and encouraged to reconsider their erroneous opinions. His own experience showed that force sometimes worked. At any rate, the threat of punishment for heresy was at least as effective as the threat of punishment for murder, which could not make a person good either. Since the visible church was a mix of good and evil anyway, only to be

---

[24] *Epistolae* 93.5.17. Quoted in Deane, *Political and Social Ideas*, 187.

[25] The Donatists were initially a movement within the church opposed to the leniency shown by the church to those who had handed over scriptures to be burnt during the Diocletian persecution of AD 303–5. They wanted to maintain a greater purity in the visible church. In the course of the fourth century they isolated themselves increasingly from the rest of the church and, when coupled with an anti-Roman cultural movement in North Africa and tacit support for guerrilla warfare against churches and cities loyal to the Catholic church, they represented a considerable threat both to public order and the unity of the Christian church.

[26] Deane, *Political and Social Ideas*, 200–202.

separated on the day of judgement, it could be maintained by force, and some good would be done in the process. Augustine overreacted to the Donatist insistence on the purity of the visible church, increasingly to emphasise its impurity and altogether earthly nature. As a consequence, the church began to look rather like a state.

The two strands of development are not contradictory, because they have in common the abandonment of idealism. The abandonment of idealism as regards the state led Augustine to emphasise the minimal, sin-restraining, functions of government; the abandonment of idealism as regards the visible church, cut away any basis for opposing state interference, should it be attempted in the name of truth. The dominant medieval reading of Augustine depended on taking his early classical views on the position of government within the natural order,[27] and combining these with his later views on the permissibility of state coercion in matters of faith. But in reconstructing Augustine's thought, we can be equally faithful by reversing the emphasis. By combining his later thought on the minimal state with his earlier position on the truly voluntary nature of the church, the essential ingredients of liberal constitutionalism are in place.

III. William of Ockham (c.1285–c.1347)

Ockham was a Franciscan philosopher and theologian who transferred from Oxford to the papal court at Avignon for uncertain reasons and fled from there with Michael of Cesena to the protection of the Holy Roman Emperor, Ludwig of Bavaria, at Munich in 1328.[28] From then on, his interest shifted dramatically from the metaphysical to the political as he was caught up in current political controversy. Broadly, Ockham addressed two issues in this second phase of his thought. First, he considered the question of the nature of apostolic poverty and the logical possibility of the Franciscan order's commitment to absolute poverty. Pope John XXII at Avignon had argued that the use of material things implied some sort of rightful ownership, to which (to cut a long story short) the Franciscan response was that there could be rightful use without ownership. Secondly, and more broadly, Ockham addressed the division of spiritual and secular power, the division between papacy and empire.

---

[27] Markus, *Saeculum*, 103.
[28] Short accounts of Ockham's life and works can be found in the introductions to his *Short Discourse on Tyrannical Government* (Cambridge, Cambridge University Press, 1992); and *Letter to the Friars Minor and Other Writings*, ed. A.S. McGrade (Cambridge, Cambridge University Press, 1995); both in the series Cambridge Texts in the History of Political Thought.

Ockham was writing against an intellectual background that was strongly monistic.[29] On the one hand there were papists or hierocrats such as James of Viterbo, Giles of Paris and the Avignonese popes who maintained the *plenitudo potestas* of the Pope. All power in earth derived from Christ through his representative, the Pope, who therefore could exercise temporal power in any matter, although it was usually delegated to others. Thus Ludwig IV at Munich was excommunicated for failing to obtain papal investiture on his election in 1314. This is sometimes referred to as a descending theory of authority.[30] On the other hand, there were the imperialists, such as (above all) Marsilius of Padua, who argued that ultimate authority resided with the community, and was granted upwards to priests and kings (ascending theory). They thus argued in Aristotelian fashion for the all-sufficing nature of the state and the supremacy of the secular power over the church.

While some argue that Ockham's political position is thoroughly secular, others have responded that it remains firmly rooted in his theology. The truth lies somewhere in between.[31] The Bible is of supreme authority for Ockham, and yet his reading of the Bible led him to insist on the validity of independent secular and ecclesiastical spheres of politics. His liberal constitutionalism,[32] with its strong dualism of church and state, is firmly rooted in the Bible. The care he takes to refute contrary arguments based on other interpretations is evidence of this respect.[33] He tended to use the New Testament literally, for example in his constant stress on texts such as 2 Timothy 2:4 ('No-one fighting for

---

[29] For background, see in particular J.A. Watt, 'Spiritual and Temporal Powers', in J.H. Burns (ed.), *The Cambridge History of Medieval Political Thought* (Cambridge, Cambridge University Press, 1988), ch. 14.

[30] For the distinction between descending and ascending medieval theories of authority, see W. Ullmann, *Principles of Government and Politics in the Middle Ages* (London, Methuen, 2nd ed., 1966).

[31] For competing interpretations of Ockham's work, see A.S. McGrade, *The Political Thought of William of Ockham* (Cambridge, Cambridge University Press, 1974), 28–43.

[32] A term adopted by E.F. Jacob in his essay *Ockham as a Political Thinker* (1936). See McGrade, *Political Thought*, 40.

[33] Many of his discussions of biblical texts were concerned to undermine the allegorical interpretations used by his opponents. For example, the reference to two swords in Luke 22:38, so often used by the papists to defend their assertion of dual jurisdiction, is demolished by showing that when taken allegorically it could refer to any two powers – or even two sets of popes, godly ones and heretics. All in all, it was better to take it literally, referring to two real swords that (almost certainly) two disciples of Jesus happened to have with them at the time. Similarly short shrift is given to the argument based on the greater and lesser lights of Gen. 1:16. See McGrade, *Short Discourse*, Bk. 5, chs. 3–6 (133–142).

God entangles himself in secular business'), and the Old Testament as a record of reliable historical events, rather than general political norms. Nevertheless, because he argues that the Bible supports a natural human understanding of liberty, property and government, it is hardly surprising that he can refer to Aristotle in support of his position. Thus natural law and divine revelation complement each other.

What were the nature and functions of church and state?[34] Just as in later Augustine, the state uses force to counteract the effects of sin. The role of government is to secure peace and justice, conceived mainly as the maintenance of public order and defence, the prosecution of crime, the protection of property and the enforcement of agreements. Although all human beings have a natural right to establish governments, the authority of government comes directly from God. Thus, apart from an initial act of popular consent in establishing government, Ockham rejects both descending and ascending theories of political authority. It is not a function of government to appoint church officials, promote true religion, virtue or the arts, because that would effectively subordinate the state to the church. Rather, laws must be framed such that individuals can choose to be virtuous (in particular, in the Franciscan case, to renounce all property). It is noticeable that nowhere does Ockham use paternal imagery to describe government. Instead, Government should be a government of free men, since this avoids despotism, and because rulers are unlikely to exceed their subjects in virtue. For example, in Book 1 of his *Short Discourse on Tyrannical Government* we find a spirited defence of freedom of thought and speech in the pursuit of truth. Perhaps, he suggests ironically, God even permitted the heresy widespread at that time to persuade experts to shake off their laziness and search divine Scripture more deeply.[35]

The church is quite different in nature, being more akin to Augustine's earlier conceptions. Unlike the state it is not primarily a legal corporation dependent for its continued existence on force and wealth. He accepts that the Pope has some limited authority in this sense, but he prefers to describe his authority as a *ministerium*, rather than *jurisdictio*. He rejects the hierocratic ideal of comprehensive spiritual direction, and instead constantly emphasises that the gospel is a law of liberty. The early church could not have welcomed freedom from the law of Moses, only to be replaced with an equally onerous law of Peter. The Pope's assertion of absolute power would make all Christians slaves, in worse bondage to law than even the Israelites.

[34] See McGrade, *Political Thought*, ch. 3.
[35] This is, of course, a classic argument of liberal thought to be echoed in Milton's *Areopagitica* 1644 ('I cannot praise a fugitive and cloistered virtue ...') (*Complete Prose Works*, London, Oxford University Press, 1959, Vol. 2, 480 ff.); and ch. 2 of J.S. Mill, *On Liberty* (1859), ed. David Spitz (New York, W.W. Norton, 1975).

This stress on liberty, both political and evangelical, is tied to a strong strand of individualism running through Ockham's work; it is sometimes suggested that he is one of the key progenitors of Western individualism. This can be seen both in his insistence that the individual will is the only truly good or bad thing (acts are only good when carried out with the right intention), and his readiness to countenance the possibility that truth does not attach to any particular office. One person may be right, and all the popes and councils of the church wrong.[36] The individual is thus both a threat and the guarantor of the political order. A threat, because in a particular case justice may reside with a few ordinary individuals, or perhaps one only, while the rest may be tyrants or heretics.[37] Yet at the same time the guarantor, for Ockham insists that it is only the virtues of individuals – their moderation, prudence, justice and courage, that enable the polity to survive.

In short, we find in Ockham a reversal of the dominant medieval reading of Augustine.[38] An ideal of a free church is coupled with a limited conception of governmental authority. Later, Ockham's writings were to become a key source for the arguments of conciliarism, the view that ultimate authority in both church and state rests with a general council or democratic assembly. The conciliarist movement in its turn was to have a profound impact on the history of European political thought. The arguments of the Paris conciliarists, pre-eminently Jean Gerson and Pierre d'Ailly in the fifteenth century, were taken up by the Spanish Dominicans and Jesuits (such as Vitoria, Molina, Suarez) in the sixteenth century, and from them to Locke.[39] It is there we must look for the roots of social contract theory and Western liberal democracy.

---

[36] This fact led Ockham constantly to stress a distinction between the regular and exceptional (*causaliter*) exercise of authority. The temporal ruler (qua Christian) may exceptionally exercise power over the Pope and vice versa.

[37] This led Antony Black to dub him 'an anti-political thinker, an anarchist individualist, a meticulous deconstructor of church and polity', *Political Thought in Europe 1250–1450* (Cambridge, Cambridge University Press, 1992), at 76.

[38] The reversal is not explicit. Ockham engages constantly with the Church Fathers, but he clearly understood Augustine's comment about bands of robbers in the traditional medieval sense (see his *Short Discourse*, Bk. 4, ch. 9, McGrade, 121–125). He draws the implication that on this account the Roman Empire had no true political authority, but characteristically follows this with an exposition of all the New Testament texts which imply that it did.

[39] See Quentin Skinner, *The Foundations of Modern Political Thought* (Cambridge, Cambridge University Press, 1978), Vol. 2, chs. 4–6.

IV. Roger Williams (c.1599–1683)

The magisterial reformers, such as Calvin, Luther and Zwingli, along with the majority of Protestant political theorists of seventeenth-century Britain, stood firmly in the medieval tradition as regards the use of state force to promote true religion and punish false. At the same time, there was a strand of thought in the seventeenth century that argued for the toleration of Trinitarian Protestant Christians, ultimately to bear fruit in the Act of Toleration 1689. And alongside this relatively conservative position, there was a minority of radical Puritans who argued for comprehensive religious toleration. Pre-eminent among these was Roger Williams.[40] Williams was ordained into the Church of England, but as a Puritan emigrated to Massachusetts Bay in the winter of 1630–31 to escape the harassment of Charles I.[41] He came increasingly to the view that the civil magistrate had no power to compel adherence to the first four commandments. He was eventually tried for undermining the authority of the magistrates and banished from the colony in 1635. In 1636 he settled in Narragansett Bay, in what was to become Providence, Rhode Island. At the time there was no thought of founding a new colony, but he required those who joined him to subscribe to two principles of government: 'that no man should be molested for his conscience', and that, 'we do promise to subject ourselves ... to all such orders or agreements as shall be made for public good of the body in an orderly way by the major consent ... only in civil things'.[42]

A number of small dissenting settlements grew up around Narragansett Bay, all committed to the principle of radical religious liberty. But doubts about the right to exercise independent civil power over the colonists, coupled with the refusal of the four surrounding colonies of Massachusetts, Plymouth, Connecticut and New Haven to recognise the independent existence of government in the area, led Williams to seek a charter from the English government in 1644. This was granted. While it says nothing about religious liberty, its silence on matters of church–state relations, dealing with civil power only, is significant. This patent was not granted by the Crown, and had to be reaffirmed in 1663 by Charles II. John Clarke, who was authorised by the Rhode Islanders to seek this renewal, summarised Williams's principles in these words: '[The people of Narragansett Bay] ... have it much in their hearts, if they be permitted, to hold forth a lively

---

[40] For the intellectual background, see John Coffey, 'Puritanism and Liberty Revisited: The Case for Toleration in the English Revolution' (1998) 41 *Historical Journal* 961.

[41] William G. McLoughlin, *Rhode Island: A Bicentennial History* (New York, W.W. Norton, 1978). Ch. 1 contains a useful summary of the early history of the colony.

[42] *Ibid*. 10.

experiment, that a flourishing and civil state may stand, yea and best be maintained, and that among English spirits, with a full liberty in religious commitments.'[43]

While in London in 1644, Roger Williams published (anonymously) a major defence of his principles of religious liberty in government in a tract entitled *The bloudy tenent of persecution*.[44] It was written in response to a tract by John Cotton, a Puritan minister in Boston, Massachusetts, who had defended the use of state force against those not adhering to the fundamentals of the Christian faith. Cotton in turn had been refuting the more radical views of John Murton expressed in a tract smuggled out of Newgate Gaol in 1620. The war of tracts between Williams and Cotton was to continue for a few more rounds, with colourful titles such as *The bloudy tenent washed and made white in the blood of the Lamb: being discussed and discharged of blood-guiltiness etc.* (Cotton, 1647), and *The Bloody tenent yet more bloody by Mr. Cotton's endeavour to wash it white in the blood of the Lamb etc.* (Williams, 1652).

While we may smile at the language, it is clear that Williams was profoundly shocked at the violence of the wars of religion that had troubled Europe for the last century or so. His opening words make this plain: 'First: that the blood of so many hundred thousand souls of protestants and papists, spilt in the wars of present and former ages, for their respective consciences, is not required nor accepted by Jesus Christ the Prince of Peace.'

The *bloudy tenent* is not a systematic work of political theory, but a passionate plea for religious liberty. Much of the argument is taken up with an exposition of key biblical verses, foremost of which is the insistence that the parable of the wheat and the tares in Matthew 13:24–30 does not refer to the church of hypocrites and true believers, but to the whole world. Thus the church – rather than the state – is to be pure, and judgement is only to be exercised on the world by God at the end of time. Consistent with this basic hermeneutic, Williams shows that Titus 3:10–11[45] does not justify the use of force against heretics, but ultimately only excommunication. And, as we might expect, there is a strong emphasis on passages such as 1 Timothy 2:1–4,[46] which is taken to limit the state to the preservation of a peaceful public order.

---

[43] Ibid. 38.
[44] Ed. Edward B. Underhill (London, Hanserd Knollys Society, 1848).
[45] Titus 3:10–11: 'Warn a divisive person once, and then warn him a second time. After that, have nothing to do with him. You may be sure that such a man is warped and sinful; he is self-condemned.'
[46] 1 Tim. 2:1–4: 'I urge, then, first of all, that requests, prayers, intercession and thanksgiving be made for everyone – for kings and all those in authority, that we may live peaceful and quiet lives in all godliness and holiness. This is good and pleases God our Saviour, who wants all men to be saved and come to a knowledge of the truth.'

Williams's argument is characterised by a strong sense of the nature of the visible church. It is to be true to its primitive form, as instituted by Christ and the apostles; it is to be pure in doctrine, discipline is to be exercised inside the church through gentle admonition, and in the last instance through excommunication, but not by any use of force. By contrast, the civil power is to preserve the peace, and only to proceed against those who use or call for violence in propagating their views. Given the context he was writing in, some of his words are shockingly radical:

> The soul that is lively and sensible of mercy received to itself in former blindness, opposition and enmity against God, cannot but be patient and gentle toward the Jews, who yet deny the Lord Jesus to be come, and justify their forefathers in Murdering of him: toward the Turks, who acknowledge Christ a great prophet, yet less than Mohamet: yea to all the several sorts of anti-Christians, who set up many a false Christ instead of him: and, lastly, to the pagans, and wildest sorts of the sons of men, who have not yet heard of the Father, nor the Son: and to all these sorts, jews, turks, anti-christians, pagans, when they oppose the light presented to them, in the sense of its own former opposition, and that God peradventure may at last give repentance.[47]

Scattered throughout the work are references that evidence a careful attempt to identify the proper scope of church and state. In response to Cotton's suggestion that it was right to punish arrogant and impetuous men, he argued that teaching alone should not count as impetuosity, even if it resulted in riot or military disaffection on the part of others.[48] There was thus to be freedom of speech.[49] Religious employment was not within the purview of the state, but secular employment was.[50] However, in contrast to the position of some radical Christians, familial relationships were subject to the authority of the magistrate, because families constituted the basic elements of society.[51]

In short, Williams assumes that a civil order is attainable between people of all faiths and none. Religious organisations could go their own way, argue, split, sue each other and dissolve, without in any way affecting the civil peace of the city: 'The church, or company of worshippers, whether true or false, is like unto a body or college of physicians in a city – like unto a corporation, society, or company of East India or Turkey merchants, or any other society or company in London.'[52]

Yet it is necessary to stress that Williams is not a modern liberal. He has a strong sense of natural morality, which it is the state's job to enforce: the

[47] *Ibid.* 64.
[48] *Ibid.* 50.
[49] *Ibid.* 141–142.
[50] *Ibid.* 132.
[51] *Ibid.* 135.
[52] *Ibid.* 46.

disobedience of children to parents, sexual immorality, drunkenness, all threatened public safety in his view and were to be punished.[53] More generally, the particular division of jurisdiction between church and state, the legitimacy of specific forms of religious association, and the areas of legal prohibition, are all thoroughly implicated in his Christianity. Williams must have assumed that the political morality he was espousing would be equally acceptable to 'jews, turks, anti-christians, pagans', but it is not clear that he espoused a theory of natural law committed to that position. Not surprisingly, given his audience, he was more concerned to show its truth by appeal to biblical revelation than natural reason.

V. Abraham Kuyper (1837–1920)

Our final example of a broadly liberal Christian political thinker is the great Dutch statesman Abraham Kuyper.[54] The neo-Calvinist intellectual movement, of which Kuyper was the leading light of his time, can, in fact, be traced back to the conversion of Groen van Prinsterer, secretary to the Dutch king, in the 1830s.[55] But it was Kuyper who turned the Dutch *reveille* into a real political force. As a theologian, politician, academic and publicist, he dominated the Dutch political and religious scene in the second half of the nineteenth century. He was the main impetus behind the founding of the Free University of Amsterdam in 1880, he was its first Professor of Theology and Rector Magnificus. He founded the Anti-Revolutionary Party, and led it for forty years, serving as Prime Minister in 1901–5. He led a major secession from the Dutch Reformed Church to form the Confederation of Reformed Churches. His views on the organisation of society and the role of government were to have a significant impact in the years 1920–60, and are still felt today.

It might seem a little perverse to call Kuyper a liberal, since one of his main opponents was the Dutch liberal party. However, the liberalism he opposed was the continental liberalism based on the rational individualism and anti-clericalism of Voltaire and Rousseau, not the Anglo-American liberalism of Montesquieu and Locke. Liberty lay at the heart of all his thought, as can be seen from the name he gave to the new university at Amsterdam, and the motto he gave to his religious periodical the *Herald*, 'a free church in a free state'. We could sum up his political philosophy as

---

[53] *Ibid.* 79.

[54] Abraham Kuyper, *Lectures on Calvinism* (Stone Lectures, 1898) (Grand Rapids, Eerdmans, 1931, 1994); Peter S. Heslam, *Creating a Christian Worldview: Abraham Kuyper's Lectures on Calvinism* (Carlisle, Paternoster Press, 1998), esp. ch. 6.

[55] Andrew Thompson, 'Christian Social and Political Thought in the Netherlands in the 19th and 20th Centuries' (unpublished lecture, Bath, Christian Studies Unit, 1975).

liberty without individualism. His approach to politics was determined by the attempt to appropriate Calvinist theology for political theory. His Calvinism led him to stress the sovereignty of God over the state, society and the church. The sovereignty of God over the state meant that he denied both theories of popular sovereignty (social contract theory) and theories of state sovereignty, such as Hegel's. He paid little attention to the classic form of government (monarchical, aristocratic, etc.) but was broadly democratic in sympathy.

The positive nature of the state can only be understood in the context of his view of society, which is one of sphere-sovereignty. Kuyper argued that different aspects, or spheres, of social existence develop spontaneously and organically, under the direct authority of God. Each sphere – family, school, church, trade union, business, scientific research – has its own logic and principles, and is independent of the others.[56] The role of government is a mechanical one designed to remedy the effects of sin. Government is not just one of the spheres of social activity alongside the others; rather it is also the sphere of spheres, committed to maintaining the independent jurisdiction of the other spheres, defending the powerless within their sphere, and raising taxes for common purposes of public order and defence. There is implicit in this a distinction between the constitution (which ensures that spheres of society do not interfere with each other) and the executive, which is the distinct sphere of government.[57]

In the context of church–state relations this means that the government should not be subject to the visible church, and should not judge between denominations – there should be religious liberty. Calvin's own view that the state should deal with false religion Kuyper opposed as a medieval hangover,[58] inconsistent with the inner logic of Calvinism, and he supported the removal of Article 36 of the Belgic Confession as a consequence. While the government members were obliged to acknowledge God as the source of their own authority, in fulfilment of that duty they were bound to their own consciences, not to the church. A Christian state might only be realised through the subjective convictions of those in authority.

The role of law in this scheme is to uphold the principles distinctive of each sphere of social existence – the problem of pluralistic society is that different worldviews tend to have different views on what those principles are. Although the matter is not entirely clear, Kuyper also used the concept of sphere-sovereignty to refer to a different stratification of

---

[56] This liberal and pluralistic view showed great affinity to the organicist thought of the German legal historian Otto von Gierke, although no relationship of dependence can be demonstrated.

[57] Lecture 3, 'Calvinism and Politics', 94.

[58] *Institutes* 4.20.9, ed. John T. McNeill (Philadelphia, The Westminster Press, 1960).

society along ideological grounds: *verzuiling*, or pillarization. On this account, the three ideological traditions of Dutch society, Roman Catholic, Calvinist and humanist were to be free to govern relations in their own spheres as they saw fit. This implied a division of society into a matrix with different social spheres on one axis and different worldviews on the other. Thus there were (and are) Roman Catholic schools, secular schools, Reformed schools, and so on. But the important point here is not his defence of religious pluralism in particular social institutions, but rather the insistence that society is divided into different activities independent from control by each other, being directly under God and the constitution.

Kuyper's intellectual work has been continued by others in the Dutch Reformed tradition, most notably in the context of political theory by Herman Dooyeweerd (1894–1977)[59] and Bernard Zylstra (1934–86). Taken together, these thinkers represent one of the most important strands of contemporary political theology.

VI. Liberal Foundations

The search for the foundations of modern liberalism is both sociological and theoretical. A number of thinkers have argued (as indeed did Kuyper) that liberalism is only able to flourish on the borrowed capital of Christian religion. While the deep divisions within Christian society from the sixteenth century onwards were a prime cause of the separation of the ecclesiastical from the political, these were divisions *within* one religion, not *about* religion. Oliver O'Donovan has recently suggested that four characteristics of the life of the Christian church were significant in the shaping of liberal society: a belief in freedom, a commitment to mercy in justice, a sense of a humane natural order, and the value of openness in speech.[60] If this sociological thesis is accepted, it would be tempting to say that liberal constitutionalism simply is the set of legal and institutional principles that emerges when the Christian church confronts Government over a sustained period of time. There is no reason to suppose that what emerges necessarily has intellectual coherence. However, as John Gray has pointed out,[61] liberal theorists have always attempted to provide

---

[59] See Herman Dooyeweerd, *The Christian Idea of the State*, tr. John Kraay (Nutley, N.J., Craig Press, 1968); idem, *A Christian Theory of Social Institutions*, tr. Magnus Verbrugge, ed. John Witte, Jr. (La Jolla, Calif., The Herman Dooyeweerd Foundation, 1986); idem, *A New Critique of Theoretical Thought*, tr. D.H. Freeman and W.S. Young (Presbyterian and Reformed Publishing, Philadelphia, 1969), Vol. 3.

[60] Oliver O'Donovan, *The Desire of the Nations: Rediscovering the Roots of Political Theory* (Cambridge, Cambridge University Press, 1996), ch. 7.

[61] John Gray, *Liberalism* (Oxford, Oxford University Press, 1986), ch. 6.

some general theoretical account of their intellectual foundations. The assumption of such theorists is that there is a coherent conception of justice, independent of the religious, moral and political divisions in society, which shows why it is right for the state to be limited according to typically liberal principles.

Gray suggests that there are broadly three strands of justification for liberal principles. First, there is the idea that liberalism is rooted in a concept of individual natural rights, which justify and limit all state action. We find this in the liberalism of, for example, Locke, Kant and Nozick. Secondly, there is John Stuart Mill's attempt to root liberal principles in utility. Finally, there is the modern contractualism of Rawls and other liberals, which seeks to derive liberal principles of justice out of ideal situations of rational decision-taking and consent.

It would be tempting to suppose that Christianity meets liberalism at the point of natural rights theory. Locke is arguably writing from within the Christian political tradition, and modern liberal Roman Catholicism rests firmly within the natural rights discourse.[62] Once one sets aside the radical denial of natural justice by reformed theologians such as Jacques Ellul[63] and Karl Barth,[64] the thinner Protestant view of natural justice seems to parallel the minimal-statism of American Christian republicanism. Thus disputes within Christianity about the extent of natural law tend to mirror disputes between egalitarian and libertarian conceptions of liberalism. But it is questionable whether this connection is the right one to pursue. Anthropology forces natural law theory from the position that certain moral rights are actually known, to the position that certain moral rights are only rationally knowable.[65] Once that move is made, natural law theory is no longer necessarily consensus-building, but shares the fate of all other rationalist attempts to ground a conception of justice. Moreover, a commitment to the existence of natural law alone is inadequate to ground a specifically liberal political theory. Most Christian theologians have held to some sort of natural law theory, as, of course, did Hobbes; it is not natural law theory that distinguishes the liberal constitutionalism of the political theorists we have been considering.

The attempt to root liberal justice in utility is widely considered to have failed, although Gray himself sought to defend Mill's reconciliation

[62] See Jacques Maritain, *Man and the State* (Chicago, University of Chicago Press, 1951); John Finnis, *Natural Law and Natural Rights* (Oxford, Clarendon Press, 1980).
[63] Jacques Ellul, *The Theological Foundation of Law*, tr. Marguerite Wieser (London, SCM Press, 1961).
[64] See esp. Karl Barth, *Church Dogmatics* (Edinburgh, T. & T. Clark, 1936–69), 3/4, §54.
[65] Margaret Mead, 'Some Anthropological Considerations Concerning Natural Law' (1961) 6 *Natural Law Forum* 51.

for a while.[66] The problem is not that the liberal constitution is not plausibly utility-maximising, but rather that the utilitarian calculus cannot determine, by itself, all the contours of the liberal constitution. Thus Ronald Dworkin has argued that while it is possible to defend a liberal conception of constitutional rights on the basis of preference-utilitarianism,[67] this in turn is more firmly grounded in a basic right to equal concern and respect. For Dworkin wants to distinguish between personal (self-regarding) and external (other-regarding) preferences, only the former of which may appear in the maximising calculus. Liberal rights are granted to counterbalance the probable appearance of other-regarding preferences in the course of majoritarian decision-taking processes. Governments should act only on the basis of what individuals want for themselves, disregarding what is wanted for others, for only in this way can they respect all people equally. At root, Dworkin's reconciliation of utility and rights is *ad hominem*, and can be treated as a procedural route to liberal principles, by which the state must be neutral between competing visions of human flourishing.

Gray himself reaches the common conclusion that it is this third route to liberal principles that holds out the most promise.[68] Procedural routes to liberalism are often structured to exclude ideals of human flourishing from being valid reasons for state action,[69] or at least to ensure that state action is neutral between ideals,[70] in an attempt to achieve widespread rational assent. This common attitude among liberals has rightly come under sustained criticism from Joseph Raz.[71] While it is true that there is likely to be more agreement about conceptions of the right than about conceptions of the good, that sociological truism does not explain why it is morally wrong to base state action on a conception of the good. The strong claim that conceptions of the good must be excluded seems to require scepticism about the rationality of conceptions of the good, which is hard to combine with a commitment to the rationality of conceptions of right. Neutrality is more plausible in its weaker claim that the state must not discriminate between citizens' conceptions of the

---

[66] John Gray, *Mill on Liberty: A Defence* (London, Routledge, 2nd ed., 1996).

[67] Ronald Dworkin, *Taking Rights Seriously* (London, Duckworth, 1977), 231–238, 272–278, 357–358.

[68] *Liberalism*, 56.

[69] John Rawls, *A Theory of Justice* (Oxford, Oxford University Press, 1972), 31. See also Bruce Ackerman, *Social Justice in the Liberal State* (London, Yale University Press, 1980), at 11: 'No reason counts as a good reason if it requires the power-holder to assert ... that his conception of the good is better than that asserted by any of his fellow-citizens.'

[70] Ronald Dworkin, 'Liberalism', in *idem*, *A Matter of Principle* (Cambridge, Mass., Harvard University Press, 1985), 191.

[71] See generally, Joseph Raz, *The Morality of Freedom* (Oxford, Clarendon Press, 1986), chs. 5, 6.

good; the problem here is that neutrality is only neutrality from a perspective informed by a vision of human flourishing. For example, one need only start considering what neutrality towards various sexual practices might mean to see its chimerical nature.

The procedures of procedural liberalism are not real procedures, but heuristic devices rationally to legitimise state action. This makes them vulnerable to two charges: first, that real people under real procedural constraints would not actually behave in the way suggested, and secondly, that the procedures have been constructed as they have been *precisely because* they will deliver the conception of substantive justice desired.

VII. Liberal Ideals

Consideration of the writers discussed in the first half of this chapter suggests that Christian liberal constitutionalism has foundations that make it distinctive from the three strands of justification just identified. While it shares with mainstream liberalism a commitment to the division of human activity into at least two realms, and while one of these realms (the 'public') is understood typically to embrace government and law, the corresponding realm is not 'private', but quintessentially the visible Christian church. Furthermore, the contours of each realm are defined in relation to the other: the church is not-state and the state is not-church. To call the non-state realm 'private', as many liberals do, is misleading if it brings with it connotations of privacy, individualism and self-fulfilment. The visible church is the body of Christ on earth, established and built by God. It is the sphere of worship, truth, beauty, moral virtue, emotional and even material support. It is fundamentally non-coercive, non-proprietary and non-legal in nature. Likewise, the state is the realm of physical well-being. It is concerned with the protection of property and persons, the enforcement of contracts, and so on. The state cannot and must not attempt to build the church, good though it undoubtedly is to build up the body of Christ, because that would deny its very nature. Nor can the church pretend to embrace all citizens and regulate matters of merely temporal concern, for then it is claiming to be the state, which it is not. As this chapter has sought to demonstrate, these themes are found at times in Augustine and lie at the centre of the thought of Ockham, Williams and Kuyper.

In placing a conception of the visible church at the heart of its political theory, Christian liberal constitutionalism is clearly idealistic. The state should be structured in a certain way so that the church may be free to live up to its ideal. And, in relying on an ideal of the visible church, liberal constitutionalism cannot be fully dependent on natural reason, but must be firmly rooted in the particular revelation of God. It is in this sense that liberalism is vulnerable and dependent on a broadly Christian social consensus.

All this is a long way from Gray's typology of liberalisms, but Gray fails to account for liberal idealism, or perfectionism. Some liberals insist that liberalism is best understood as having its own ideals, its own virtues, its own conception of community and the good life.[72] The acceptance that liberalism might be built around a specific ideal of human flourishing both dethrones and strengthens liberal theories of justice. They are dethroned as arbiters between competing conceptions of human flourishing and instead become contenders themselves as correct conceptions of human flourishing. But at the same time they are strengthened, not only because they accept the force of critiques of liberal neutrality, but because they give public officials a positive vision of human flourishing that limits their power.

Once one accepts the need to identify a liberal ideal that can inform public policy, the question simply becomes which ideal best expresses the liberal tradition, showing why and how law is to be limited. The ideal of the autonomous individual is the most obvious candidate. The point of Hart's well-known defence of a private sphere of morality[73] was not to justify licentious behaviour, but to give the individual a chance for responsible moral choice. Of course, one cannot force people to be free, but the recognition that government has some responsibility in creating the conditions for individual autonomy allows one to legitimise restrictions on activities that undermine autonomy.[74] Thus where anti-perfectionist liberals such as David Richards tend to argue in favour of derestricting autonomy-reducing behaviour,[75] perfectionists allow the state a role in fostering the conditions of ongoing autonomy. Furthermore, although there is a longstanding connection between liberalism and individualism, recent liberal writing is modifying that position in the face of communitarian challenge.[76] Given that an autonomous individual cannot exist in isolation, but requires both material conditions and liberating personal relationships to flourish, is it

---

[72] *Ibid.*; Will Kymlicka, *Liberalism, Community and Culture* (Oxford, Clarendon Press, 1989); Stephen Macedo, *Liberal Virtues* (Oxford, Clarendon Press, 1991); William Galston, *Liberal Purposes* (Cambridge, Cambridge University Press, 1991).

[73] H.L.A. Hart, *Law, Liberty and Morality* (Oxford, Oxford University Press, 1963).

[74] Raz, *Morality of Freedom*, chs. 14, 15.

[75] See David A.J. Richards, *Sex, Drugs, Death and the Law: An Essay on Decriminalization and Human Rights* (Totowa, N.J., Rowman & Littlefield, 1982).

[76] The most accessible account of the debate between liberals and communitarians is Stephen Mulhall and Adam Swift, *Liberals and Communitarians* (Oxford, Blackwell, 2nd ed., 1996). For an example of a liberal appropriation of communitarian concerns, see Ronald Dworkin, *Law's Empire* (London, Fontana, 1986), 195–215.

not more accurate to say that the liberal ideal is that of an individual in relationship with others committed in a non-coercive way to mutual material and emotional support, and the common pursuit of truth, goodness and beauty? In short, does not the ideal of the Christian church fit rather well?

There is one obvious way in which the ideal of the Christian church can provide us with a more robust liberalism. It concerns the impermissibility of coercion in matters of conscience. Locke, of course, argued for religious toleration on the grounds that the magistrate could not change the human understanding of religious truth.[77] Kymlicka gives the typical liberal strengthened version of that argument by insisting that a life is only worth leading if it is led 'from the inside': 'Praying to God may be a valuable activity, but you have to believe that it's a worthwhile thing to do … You can coerce someone into going to church and making the right physical movements, but you won't make someone's life better that way.'[78]

Locke agreed, although for specifically Christian reasons, but the issue is not whether coerced religious worship is valueless from every perspective, secular or religious. Augustine believed as fervently as any modern liberal in the independence of the human intellect from direct external human pressure. Only God could change the mind. Yet he also recognised the truth that external circumstances do, to some extent, affect the way we think. To put it bluntly, forcing people into church can, to some extent, work, in the sense that some may eventually come voluntarily to accept the value of what they have hitherto involuntarily been forced to do. If liberalism is not to fall back on scepticism about the good (perhaps praying to God isn't valuable after all) it needs to know why a community of people praying to God, among whom some are there by force, is morally unacceptable, given *ex hypothesi* that it is good to pray to God and that by being there some of the unwilling participants may in time come to accept that fact. The sort of strong defence of religious liberty that the liberal is committed to needs a conception of the non-coercive religious community as ideal.

The ideal of the Christian church is not only theoretically necessary to give shape to the limitation of the state; it is also one which, to the extent that it is lived out by Christians, forces the state into a liberal mould. For the first allegiance of Christians is to a universal moral community, which the state is prevented from promoting and powerless to prohibit.

---

[77] See John Horton and Susan Mendus, *John Locke: A Letter Concerning Toleration in Focus* (London, Routledge, 1991), for Locke's text; and also Jeremy Waldron, 'Locke: Toleration and the Rationality of Persecution', at 98. Waldron argues that Locke's case for the valuelessness of coerced religious worship is itself religiously specific, at 117.

[78] Kymlicka, *Liberalism*, 12.

VIII. Liberal Principles

The conclusion of this train of thought may be uncomfortable, but it is not really surprising. The attempt to identify general theoretical foundations for liberal principles of justice leads back to a thoroughly contentious ideal. One can understand why Rawls abandoned the view that his account of justice was rationally comprehensive, accepting instead that it was a purely political conception of justice around which an overlapping consensus could form.[79] Rawls now accepts that within liberal constitutionalism greater diversity can be found at the level of its theoretical foundations than about its basic principles. However, he suggests that this does not matter, so long as we can converge on principles of political morality. If Rawls is right, the only significance of the thesis of this chapter is academic and apologetic. But regardless of whether liberalism is dependent on a specific religious ideal for its intellectual coherence, as I have argued, the choice of foundations does indeed impact on the detail of policy. While at one level 'we are all liberals now', our liberalisms have different countenances according to their parentage.[80] A Christian liberalism will not deliver precisely the same constitutional structure and political programme as its secular counterpart.

The consequences of adopting the Christian church as the liberal ideal are many and various.[81] A few examples spring readily to mind, and will have to suffice here. To quote Stephen Macedo again: 'Liberalism holds out the promise, or the threat, of making all the world like California. By encouraging tolerance or even sympathy for a wide array of lifestyles and eccentricities, liberalism creates a community in which it is possible to decide next week I might quit my career in banking, leave my wife and children, and join a Buddhist cult.'[82] Given that he insists elsewhere, as all liberals must, that freedom includes the freedom to enter into binding commitments, one can query whether the liberty to abandon wife and children is really required by liberal principles. The point that the Christian liberal can make is that certain conceptions of marriage (but by no means all) are liberating in spite of the ongoing commitment they need to support them. The state may legitimately foster such conceptions of marriage.

---

[79] John Rawls, *Political Liberalism* (New York, Columbia University Press, 1993).

[80] Waldron makes exactly the same point in 'Locke', 114.

[81] For a discussion of the impact of a theologically informed conception of democracy on the question of constitutional review see Robert Song, *Christianity and Liberal Society* (Oxford, Clarendon Press, 1997), ch. 6. See also my 'A Bill of Rights for the United Kingdom?' in Paul Beaumont (ed.), *Christian Perspectives on Law Reform* (Carlisle, Paternoster, 1998), 25–50.

[82] Stephen Macedo, *Liberal Virtues*, 278.

To take another example, if one accepts that the soundest foundation for a liberal constitution may be found in the ideal of the visible church, certain forms of religious establishment may justly mark up the state's symbolic commitment to, and dependence on, Christianity. Such establishments must not jeopardise the freedom of the church to be the church, or force non-members into membership, but this does not rule out every imaginable establishment. Or again, Kymlicka suggests that Rawls appears unable in his recent writing to explain why individuals should not bind themselves into communities or religious commitments from which they can no longer rescind; in short, why freedom of conscience could not be alienated.[83] The inalienability of freedom of conscience is required by the ideal of a church freely joined and freely adhered to. Many Islamic countries deny that the right to freedom of religion includes the right to change religion, rendering the matter controversial within international law, and its resolution by liberal lawyers significant.

The division of jurisdiction between church and state cannot be clean, since all of life is properly an act of worship and is simultaneously rooted in the physical conditions of human existence. Liberal constitutionalism is a compromise built on the now-and-not-yet of the Kingdom of Christ. Thus, while we can identify points of human activity that are clearly nothing to do with the state qua state (forms of worship) or the church qua church (size of defence budget), other areas hang awkwardly in between. Education is perhaps currently the most contentious, although the employment rights of religious workers and the control of religious property can raise equally tricky issues. The danger of anti-idealistic, and even natural rights-based, liberalisms is that they regulate these areas as if they fell only in the competence of the state, failing to see the religious interest. If the state wishes to establish institutions that pursue truth, it must also recognise that the pursuit of truth is not primarily a governmental responsibility.[84]

IX. Conclusions

Rather than rejecting liberalism on account of the defects of its current deviant form, there is an urgent need for Christians to reclaim it. Much modern liberal political thought is agnostic on matters of faith and morality, suspecting that commitment to a particular moral and religious tradition is incompatible with personal self-fulfilment and the toleration

---

[83] Kymlicka, *Liberalism*, 59–61.

[84] For a consideration of some of the overlapping spheres of church and state, see my 'Religious Liberty as a Collective Right', in Andrew Lewis and Richard O'Dair (eds.), *Law and Religion* (Oxford, Oxford University Press, 2001).

of others.[85] This risks the exclusion of religious concerns from all public life, and undermines existing forms of social cohesion. It risks ultimately destroying the civic virtues that make political liberalism possible.[86]

The blood of the martyrs was not only the seed of the church, but also the seed of the liberal state. Christians can legitimately claim to have both a principled foundation for liberal constitutionalism and the spiritual resources to sustain it. The motive force behind that commitment to the basic contours of the liberal constitution is not merely a sense of natural justice based on a common humanity, but on the calling of the visible church – a real and present human institution – to witness to the Kingdom of Christ, which is not of this world. There is no more radical motive for limiting law.

---

[85] See Kent Greenawalt, *Religious Convictions and Political Choice* (New York, Oxford University Press, 1988)

[86] Jonathan Sacks, *The Politics of Hope* (London, Vintage/Ebury, 1997), has mounted a recent and brilliant defence of this point.

2

The Legal Framework for Religion in Schools in England and Wales: Enforcement or Enablement?

David Harte

I. Introduction

Religion in schools is an area where Christians have a vested interest and it involves unavoidable tension with contemporary society, which is not explicitly Christian.[1] The topic is an appropriate one for questioning the proper limits of the law from a Christian perspective. It raises a number of interesting general issues. But it is also of great practical importance for the future character of Britain and for the welfare of children, not least those from Christian homes. It is therefore vital for Christians to articulate their position in contending for proper legal rules with regard to the place of religion in schools, even though those may conflict with principles professed by other ideologies such as secular liberalism.[2] It is important, however, that care should be taken not to assume the rightness of a privileged position for religion, and specifically the Christian faith, within the school system. Equally, though, it is important not to evade a proper responsibility for advancing Christian values, out of a fear of seeming triumphalist.

---

[1] The significance of the topic was recognised by Paul Beaumont in the second volume in this series: 'Liberals are in danger of making equality of treatment an absolute and thereby becoming intolerant of those who think there are higher values at stake, e.g. insisting that church schools should employ non-Christians as teachers or forcing such schools into the private sector' (Introduction in *Christian Perspectives on Human Rights and Legal Philosophy*, ed. Paul R. Beaumont (Carlisle, Paternoster, 1998), 3).

[2] *Ibid.* at 34, where Ian Leigh points out that 'Liberal attitudes towards individual autonomy may ... clash with such belief systems [as those emphasised by Protestants which may be connected with certain of the principles of John Locke including personal moral responsibility, individual salvation and the importance of a personal response and commitment to God] with regard to the approach they would take on religious education and upbringing of children, who may be treated as autonomous individuals by Liberals earlier (or later) than they are by their parents.'

This chapter starts with a brief explanation of the legal place afforded to religion, and specifically to Christianity, in the English and Welsh school systems. Then, a general comparison is drawn between the use of the law to enforce particular standards and its use as a means of enabling or facilitating human liberty and fulfilment. The relevance of this distinction is then discussed more fully with regard to the three distinct levels at which religion is given a place by law in schools; in the provisions for religious education, in the requirement of times for worship during the school day, and in the retention within the state system of schools with a specifically religious ethos. There is considerable disagreement between Christians as well as among others over the legal provision for religion in schools. However, it is suggested that if the law is seen in terms of enablement rather than enforcement this may offer insight into how different approaches may be accommodated both here and in other contexts.

II. The Legal Place of Religion in English and Welsh Schools Today

The first level at which religious belief is recognised in the legal framework for school education in England[3] is its ring-fencing as a subject for study in ordinary state schools. The principle of compulsory provision of religious instruction was established when the modern pattern of universal state education was set up under the Education Act 1944. The legal requirement for a general National Curriculum was not imposed until 1988 and until then religion was the one subject that had to be offered in state schools,[4] although its content was determined locally.

---

[3] As with most areas of law, even before devolution of law-making powers to the Scottish Parliament under the Scotland Act 1998, Scottish education law and the Scottish educational system differed markedly from those in southern Britain. In Scotland most denominational, voluntary schools transferred to the state system under the Education (Scotland) Act 1872 and the Education (Scotland) Act 1918. Such schools have, in theory, been permitted to continue a religious ethos, and there is a duty for schools to be provided to take account of the religious beliefs of parents (Education (Scotland) Act 1980, s. 17 (2)). In Scottish schools, religious instruction is given by teachers appointed by the local authority but in denominational schools they must be approved 'as regards their religious belief and character' by representatives of the relevant denomination (*ibid.* s. 21). The local education authority must also appoint an unpaid supervisor of religious instruction for each such school approved by the denomination, with power to enter the school at will and a duty to report to the authority on 'the efficiency of religious instruction' there.

[4] Education Reform Act 1988, s. 2, now Education Act 1996, s. 353.

Today the National Curriculum and locally determined religious education together make up the 'basic curriculum' all state schools must provide.[5]

Religious education varies between those schools with a specific religious ethos and those without such an ethos. Confessional schools either use the local authority 'agreed syllabus' or are left to follow their own arrangements.[6] This usually means the syllabus of the local Church of England or Roman Catholic diocese. The local authority 'agreed syllabus' is used in the normal 'community school', which is not a religious foundation and is not attached to a religious denomination. The 'agreed syllabus' is made by the local education authority syllabus conference.[7] This conference comprises four 'committees', namely separate representatives from (1) faith bodies, including Christian denominations other than the Church of England; (2) in England but not Wales, the Church of England; (3) teachers' representatives; and (4) the local authorities' own representatives. The first group does not include representatives of the Church of England since they have their own committee. In Wales, as there is no separate group for the disestablished Church in Wales, it is represented by the general faith committee. A majority of each of the statutory groups must agree a syllabus before it can be adopted by the local education authority.[8]

Local education authorities are required to review their syllabuses for religious education by convening syllabus committees, 'from time to time'.[9] In addition, each local education authority must maintain a Standing Advisory Council on Religious Education (SACRE) to advise on religious education and worship. This is constituted with subcommittees representing the same groups as a syllabus committee.[10]

A fundamental requirement of each agreed syllabus is that it 'shall reflect the fact that the religious traditions in Great Britain are in the main Christian whilst taking account of the teaching and practices of the other principal religions represented in Great Britain'. This provision, which is now in the Education Act 1996, s. 375 (3), was introduced by the Education Act 1988, following a struggle between Christians, who were concerned that pluralism had diluted the position of Christianity in the classroom, and secularists, who wanted religion excluded altogether.[11]

---

[5] See Education Act 1996, s. 352 (1) (a) and School Standards and Framework Act 1998, s. 69 and Sched. 19. As to local syllabuses see Education Act 1996, Sched. 31.

[6] School Standards and Framework Act 1998, s. 69 and Sched. 19.

[7] Education Act 1996, s. 375 and Sched. 31.

[8] Ibid. Sched. 31, para. 4 (6), para. 10 (2) (a).

[9] Ibid. Sched. 31, para. 2.

[10] Ibid. s. 390.

[11] Education Reform Act 1988, s. 8 (3). For an analysis of the Parliamentary debates see Colin Alves, 'Just a Matter of Words? The Religious Education

The idea that religious education should be a required part of the state basic curriculum seems, at present, to be generally accepted. Even the highlighting of Christianity was eventually done in a manner that headed off controversy, mainly owing to the intervention in the House of Lords of the then Bishop of London, Dr Graham Leonard.[12] Nevertheless, the exact meaning of the standard by which religious education syllabuses are to be judged remains contentious.

The second level recognising the importance of religion in the legal framework for English and Welsh schools is the enshrinement of worship in the ordinary school day. Under the Education Act 1944, a single act of worship was to be provided for all the pupils at each state school at the beginning of each school day. Problems of limited accommodation in schools led to the rule being adapted so that sessions may now be held at different times during the school day and for different groups. However, under the School Standards and Framework Act 1998, s. 70. the basic requirement remains that schools must provide daily worship for every pupil.

Tucked away in Schedule 20 of the 1998 Act is crucial detail on the form of worship in non-confessional schools.[13] By paragraph 3 (2) 'the required collective worship shall be wholly or mainly of a broadly Christian character'. It is further provided that 'collective worship is of a broadly Christian character if it reflects the broad traditions of Christian belief without being distinctive of any particular Christian denomination'.[14] Not every act of collective worship need comply with sub-paragraph (2) 'provided that taking any school term as a whole, most such acts which take place in the school do comply'.[15]

The third level at which the place of religion is protected within the state school system is where specifically religious schools, sometimes referred to as denominational or confessional schools, are given a place where their own ethos is guaranteed. This is not simply a matter of parents being free to opt out of the state system and to send their children to private denominational schools if they can afford to pay. Religious denominations that participate in the state education system, and especially the Church of England, are seen as partners with the state and the state accepts the liability for underwriting most of the cost of denominational schools within the state school system.

---

[11] *(continued)* Debate in the House of Lords' (1991) 13 *British Journal of Education* 168–174. For further references see J.D.C. Harte, 'The Religious Dimension of the Education Reform Act 1988' (1989) 1 *Ecclesiastical Law Journal* (5)32–52; and John M. Hull, 'Religious Education and Christian Values in the Education Reform Act 1988' (1990) 2 *Ecclesiastical Law Journal* 69.

[12] Parliamentary Debates, HL, 16 May 1998, col. 14.

[13] Introduced through the Education Reform Act 1988, s. 6.

[14] School Standards and Framework Act 1998, Sched. 20, para. 3 (3).

[15] *Ibid.* para. 3 (4).

In England and Wales there is a deeply established historical distinction between ordinary state schools and church schools. In 1944 a majority of schools were run by the Church of England, and a significant number by the Roman Catholic Church. These schools were absorbed into the new national system based on local authorities, which was set up by the Education Act 1944. It was of great significance that church schools were allowed to retain their denominational identity and ethos. There was a distinction between voluntary aided schools and voluntary controlled schools. In aided schools the denomination accepted responsibility for 15 per cent of the capital costs of the building and in return had greater control over religious education and worship.[16]

Since 1944 the picture has changed and there is a far smaller proportion of church schools, although still a substantial number at primary school level. Most of these are still attached to the Church of England. However, at secondary level there are relatively few church schools and most of these are Roman Catholic.[17]

By the School Standards and Framework Act 1998 the Blair Government has stamped its mark on the English and Welsh school system. In particular, it has renamed ordinary state schools as 'Community' rather than 'County' schools, emphasising their importance as a focus for the surrounding community, for example, in making available their facilities for others and stressing the value of involvement by the local community in school activities.[18]

The Thatcher Government had created a new category of grant maintained schools funded directly by central government rather than local authorities. These could have a religious foundation, but changes from local authority to maintained religious schools were unpopular with the main churches because they could develop independence from denominations as well as from local authorities. Maintained schools have now largely been brought back into the local authority ambit, although with more control over their own character, as 'foundation schools'.

Initial plans of the Blair Government had indicated that church schools would also lose part of their existing independence.[19] Following consultation, there was a major change of policy. The School Standards and Framework Act 1998, as enacted, recognises especially the Church of England and the Roman Catholic Church as major partners with local authorities in providing good education. The distinction between voluntary aided and voluntary controlled schools is continued. Since 1944 there have been a small number of Methodist and Jewish schools.

---

[16] *Ibid.* Sched. 3, para. 5.
[17] Annual *Statistics of Education: Schools in England,* Department for Education and Employment. See too John Gay, *The Geographical Distribution of Church Schools in England* (Abingdon, Culham College Institute, 2000).
[18] School Standards and Framework Act 1998, s. 20.
[19] The White Paper *Excellence in Schools*, 1997, Cm. 3681.

Strikingly, other minority faiths, particularly Islam, are now being allowed their own schools. At the same time, controlled church schools are able to opt for greater freedom, as aided schools and community schools may opt to become voluntary schools with a religious ethos.[20] There is an atmosphere in which new church schools, especially secondary schools, have become a prospect.[21]

It is important to note that there are conscience provisions for both children, or rather their parents,[22] and teachers[23] who want to opt out from either religious education or worship in any state school, although in the case of teachers these are much weaker in voluntary aided schools. This aspect of the legislation, which is considered more fully below, demonstrates the practical importance of limiting the use of the law to impose Christian values where these no longer enlist general support in society. It also illustrates that framing the law to enable schools to provide a Christian ethos requires that the law should not enforce that ethos against the will of parents or teachers. An aspect of the Christian ethos may be seen as protection of the religious freedom of all citizens.

III. Enforcement and Enablement as Two Faces to Law

In general terms, law may either be coercive, enforcing certain rules by means of a battery of sanctions,[24] or it may be enabling, designed to help people to run their lives in a fuller, more satisfying manner.[25] A coercive system of law is designed to enforce certain patterns of behaviour,

---

[20] School Standards and Framework Act 1998, s. 35 and Sched. 8.
[21] General Synod *Church of England Schools in the New Millennium* (GS 1321/1998).
[22] School Standards and Framework Act 1998, s. 71.
[23] *Ibid.* ss. 59 and 60.
[24] A recent analysis of the manner in which law may be coercive has been provided by Grant Lamond, 'The Coerciveness of Law' (2000) 20 *Oxford Journal of Legal Studies* 39–62.
[25] The concept of 'enabling' used here may be contrasted with more ideologically explicit approaches to the development of modern secular law such as 'liberalising', which is concerned to maximise individual autonomy, and 'mobilising', which is concerned to promote social engineering in accordance with some political design; see Anthony Allot, *Limits of the Law* (London, Butterworth, 1980), 178–179. A notion that may be compared with 'enablement' in the sense discussed here is that of 'facilitating'. Facilitative law may be said to make it easier for things to be done, as where education law facilitates the ease with which local authorities may ensure the education of the population. However, it does not necessarily imply the widening of opportunities for fulfilment by individuals, as does the concept of enablement.

irrespective of the wishes of those affected. Indeed, it is based on the assumption that people will not willingly pursue the behaviour that the law is framed to enforce. By contrast, an enabling system of law prescribes norms that enable people to conduct their affairs consistently in accordance with recognised principles. It assists them in making their own choices and will tend to allow a range of options, even if there is a standard pattern of behaviour recognised as the norm.

These two models merge with one another and most bodies of legal rules can be analysed from either perspective. Some laws fit much more convincingly into one model or the other, but the distinction is useful in questioning what the primary purpose of a particular rule or principle is and how it may best be achieved.

In the wide field of public law, the criminal law is obviously concerned essentially with enforcing particular standards of behaviour on individuals in the public interest. At the other extreme, rights in public law to state benefits, such as housing or welfare payments, are designed to enable the needy in society. Education law straddles the two extremes. It involves a duty under which parents must either provide education for their children or submit to it being imposed upon them by the state.[26] On the other hand, parents on behalf of their children have extensive rights; notably the right to state education in the first place, since most parents want their children educated and see state provision as a right rather than a matter of duty on their part.[27]

The subject of religion in schools is a microcosm illustrating the two approaches of enforcing and enabling. Some parents who see education in general as a right may regard the religious element as something of an imposition. Others see it as a vital part of the right for their children to be educated. Where the religious provision in schools meets the expectations of Christian parents, they will fear its removal and the prospect of state education assuming a much more threatening nature, as a system for imposing an alien secular culture and sub-Christian or anti-Christian values. By contrast, some Christian parents take the view that religion in schools is now often presented by non-Christian teachers who misrepresent the content of the faith and may have the effect of inoculating children against it. Like secular parents who object to religion in schools altogether, such Christian parents may choose to exercise their rights to withdraw their children.

Ultimately, enforcement is not for its own sake but to protect the rights of those who might otherwise be injured or deprived. These include those against whom the enforcement is directed. If he beats up other children, a bully may be punished, to guide him to a more fulfilled

---

[26] Education Act 1996, s. 7.
[27] This approach is reinforced by the First Protocol to the European Convention on Human Rights, which recognises the right to education.

life, as well as to make life easier for the victims in future.[28] Equally, even a law clearly designed to enable or facilitate must be backed up by sanctions or it will not work, though the sanctions are a last resort.[29] Thus the system of schools law in its entirety is designed to enable all children to have the opportunity to learn, both for its own sake and to equip them for living. However, if parents fail to cooperate and keep their children away from school, while not providing alternative suitable education, they may be forced to comply or lose custody of their children to the local authority.[30]

Thus, a body of law may be essentially enabling, but it may be framed within a system of imposed state provision, which therefore seems to be an enforcement system. In such a case, the enabling element may be reinforced by legal privilege, such as the power to opt out of a normative situation. In the specific matter of religious education this privilege is illustrated by the freedom for parents to withdraw their children.[31]

Enabling law may, also, involve extensive duties on public bodies responsible for providing a public service. Here, there may also be provision for conscientious opting out by individuals, such as teachers choosing not to take part in religious education.[32] However, significantly, a local education authority itself has no right to deny a parent or teacher the exercise of their power to withdraw. Nor can it opt out from its own duties.[33] Thus an English local education authority has

[28] The justification for punishment has generated an immense body of literature. At one end of the spectrum punishment may be justified in biblical terms on the basis of retribution. However, even retribution may be seen as supporting the value of individual offenders as persons by emphasising their autonomy and right to make moral choices; see the influential article by C.S. Lewis, 'The Humanitarian Theory of Punishment' (autumn 1948–49) 3(3) *20th Century* 5–12. See too Herbert L. Packer, *The Limits of the Criminal Sanction* (Stanford, Stanford University Press, 1969).

[29] The point may be illustrated by the use of injunctions to support various regulatory controls. The sanction under the regulatory system may be strengthened if an injunction is used to deter an individual who seems intent on breaking the regulation. Disobedience of the injunction may be punished as contempt of court with the sanction of imprisonment; e.g. *Kent County Council v Batchelor (No. 2)* [1979] 1 WLR 213.

[30] Children Act 1989, s. 36.

[31] School Standards and Framework Act 1998, s. 71. The enforcement framework will ensure that the children who are withdrawn will be required to do something else during the allotted time.

[32] *Ibid.* ss. 59 and 60.

[33] In Hohfeldian terms, the local education authority is under a liability to accept the exercise of a power by the parent or teacher but it has a disability from declining to provide religious education; Walter Wheeler Cook (ed.), *Fundamental Legal Conceptions as Applied in Judicial Reasoning by: Wesley Newcomb Hohfeld* (New Haven, Yale University Press, 1919).

no power to choose not to offer religious education, for example on the grounds that its elected members are against religion.[34]

Although a system designed to enable members of the public imposes unavoidable duties on public officers and elected bodies, it may confer considerable discretion. In education law this may include extensive powers to override parental wishes. If religious education in state schools is seen essentially as a means to enable families to benefit from exposure to the Christian faith, where the discretion is exercised by officers or elected councillors who are unsympathetic to Christianity, the system may appear more arbitrary and difficult for parents to control by legal means than one where a clear and specifically Christian ethos was being imposed. Two examples of where these tensions may arise are the complex but finely balanced words providing for both religious education and worship in English non-denominational schools, discussed more fully below.

The distinction between law for enforcing values and law for enabling or facilitating the improvement of life may be considered to reflect the fundamental contrast between law and grace. The Old Testament Law was designed to impose godly standards. Jewish teachers, before and since Jesus Christ's earthly ministry, added a mass of detailed rules to provide guidance for a way of living within the principles enshrined by the Law of the Torah, the books of Moses. Some of these codes, notably the dietary laws, were themselves contained in the Pentateuch.[35] As the aim of all this was God's loving will to help his people to live in harmony with himself, Jesus naturally explained that he had come to fulfil rather than to destroy the Law,[36] and principles of ethics based on the New as well as the Old Testament were developed by the church over the centuries and expressed as canon law.

Within the Reformed tradition, there has been a tendency to question canon law as a reversion to Old Testament legalism.[37] Those living by the Law could easily miss its purpose and treat it simply as a mass of rules to be obeyed for their own sake. The reformers of the sixteenth and seventeenth centuries therefore emphasised strongly how the new covenant of the gospel had superseded the old covenant of the Law. However, if the distinction between enforcement and enablement is maintained, it may be better understood how the new covenant of grace does not so much

---

[34] In Scotland the religious character of a school may be terminated only on the express authority of a local referendum (Education (Scotland) Act 1980, s. 8).

[35] E.g. Lev. 11.

[36] Matt. 5:17.

[37] Significant here is the writing of Rudolf Sohm, particularly his *Kirchenrecht* (Munich, Duncker & Humblot, 1923). For discussion of this see A.V. Dulles, *Models of the Church* (Dublin, Gill & Macmillan, 1976); and Norman Doe, 'Towards a Critique of the Role of Theology in English Ecclesiastical and Canon Law' (1993) 2 *Ecclesiastical Law Journal* 328. See too Wilhelm Steinmuller 'Divine Law and its Dynamism in Protestant Theology of Law' (1969) 8(5) *Concilium* 13.

abolish the Law of the old covenant as transform it. Thus, instead of a form of bondage to impossible standards, it has become a system for enabling the living out of the Christian life. Examples of modern law, both within the church and nationally, need to be seen in this light if their proper limits are to be considered.[38]

IV. The Utility of the Distinction Between Law as Enforcement and Law as Enablement

In defining a Christian perspective on law, it is normal to emphasise differences from other ideologies. In practice, the similarities also need to be recognised. Similarities between theological and secular aims are fundamental to any concept of natural law that may be discovered by reason rather than by revelation.[39] Recognition of what the two approaches have in common is essential if an effective Christian contribution is to be made in shaping law for the future. Consistency between Christian principle and what is recognised as right by those who are trying to do good in the world independently of revelation provides the chemistry for the salt of the gospel to be absorbed into the world, so that the gospel may have practical effect.[40]

---

[38] For a discussion of the limitations of law as a tool for social control see Iredell Jenkins, *Social Order and the Limits of Law: A Theoretical Essay* (Princeton, Princeton University Press, 1980). In particular Jenkins argues that historically law has developed from a natural law perspective emphasising status of the individual and corresponding duties within a divinely given social order, through a phase emphasising individual autonomy and individual rights, to the situation where the individual may be seen as a hapless victim of a complex and overwhelming economic system. Here the law emphasises underlying human rights that redress the balance between competing interests which tend to defeat all individual aspirations. In this context law tends to dominate over other social forces and systems, including religion. However, in doing so it tends to distort and dehumanise the support it is intended to provide both for individuals and for the general public good. Jenkins argues that to achieve its proper purpose law must exert its supremacy but 'it must accept these other forces as allies in a common undertaking and support them in their distinctive roles' (372).

[39] Rom. 2:12–16.

[40] In Romans 2 Paul indicates that doing good in this context means acting in accordance with the law. The principle that may be agreed here between Christians and others is that of loving one's neighbour as oneself (Lev. 19:18; Matt. 5:43; 19:19; Mark 12:31; Luke 10:27; Rom. 13:9; Gal. 5:14; Jas. 2:8). What loving one's neighbour as oneself means in a particular context will not of course always be obvious and Christians will disagree between themselves as well as with others.

A label that, notoriously, needs to be handled with care is the term 'liberal'. In particular, it may mean different things in a theological as opposed to a political context. Philosophically, there may be a tendency to identify liberalism with secularism and a liberal ethos, at a certain level, may indeed seem incompatible with the certainties of a faith centred on the sure conviction expressed in Jesus through the pages of the New Testament. However, a consistent liberalism must be agnostic rather than secular. As Ian Leigh has clearly demonstrated, those holding a liberal position run the risk of shooting themselves in the foot if they claim some underlying authority for their own position that they deny to others.[41]

In an honest attempt not to allow things to slide into anarchy, the liberal will have recourse to the rule of law, as it is modified through the democratic process. Then, if one person's freedom must submit to someone else's, the ballot box is at least better than a lottery or the rule of brute force. For example, in the strained circumstances of Northern Ireland, it might be argued that a majority of votes demanding the abolition of sectarian schools would justify a system of entirely secular schooling.[42] However, the genuine liberal aim would seem to be to avoid such absolutes if at all possible and to maximise choice. This contrasts with the aim of the secularist who masquerades under the title of liberal and seeks to banish religion from schools by demanding a spurious neutrality, which is really a thinly disguised atheism.

The agnostic liberal, it is suggested, should at least tolerate a religious dimension in schools. If a large proportion of parents want a place for religion in the school, the logic must be to let them have it, provided the sensibilities of others are respected. In terms of maximising both choice and the information needed for making choices freely, the agnostic liberal should favour the availability of religion in schools. It is a subject of wide interest and irrespective of whether or not a person believes it to be objectively true, the major religions and especially Christianity, have features widely recognised by non-believers as supporting the social good.[43] For those with a living faith, religion is of the greatest importance

---

[41] Ian Leigh, 'Towards a Christian Approach to Religious Liberty', in Beaumont, *Christian Perspectives on Human Rights and Legal Philosophy*. See J. Rivers, chapter 1 in this volume, for an attempt to locate Christian political and legal thought within a liberal framework.

[42] In practice any such agreement by the electorate would seem highly improbable. The abolition of religion in schools is more likely by a secular majority wishing to impose their will on a religious minority. A Christian minority might consider it right to accept the democratic decision even though it believed it both wrong and unfair. However, if a majority of one religion were to seek to abolish schooling provided for a minority of another religion that would seem to be a recipe for civil disorder.

[43] This statement could be contested by the atheist and criticisms of harm done in the name of religion must be taken seriously. However, such harm

and, thus, it may be argued that it should be given a place both for their sake as citizens with their own rights and also so that the indifferent will be encouraged to recognise and respect its importance for those who do believe.

On the other hand, if religion is given a legally guaranteed place in schools, the appropriate nature of that place remains contentious. As discussed below, there is a preliminary question as to what subjects, if any, should be enforced on individual pupils, rather than simply being made available. Also, if religion is given a guaranteed place it will be necessary for the law to make clear what it comprises, in particular to what extent there should be an obligation to provide treatment of religious belief and the experience of worship, specifically of Christian belief and worship, rather than merely some basic principles of morality and spiritual awareness that might be shared with other faiths and with secular humanists under a general blanket of citizenship and aesthetics.

Christians may differ among themselves over how far God-approved behaviour should be enforced, but, so far as is feasible in any particular society, the liberating character of the New Testament may be said to encourage maximum variety. The Christian with liberal tendencies may be concerned not to impose views on others, but, if the legal provisions for religion in schools are seen as enabling rather than enforcing, they may more readily be appreciated in terms of opportunities and rights for those who want them rather than as a bundle of restrictions and duties.

It must be recognised here that some Christians, particularly those of more independent and nonconformist traditions, may be deeply suspicious of religious education or worship enforced on individuals or even made available in ordinary schools. Historically, nonconformist experience of domination by the national church led to the provision in the 1944 Act that prevented the use of denominational creeds in non-denominational schools. Today the fear may be rather that a theologically liberal or syncretistic treatment of Christianity in schools will either breed a form of heretical belief or may inoculate children against true belief or indeed destroy any interest in religion. The logic of this position may be to aim at eliminating any formal treatment of religion, especially worship, from ordinary state schools, and to confine it to specifically confessional schools.

---

[43] *(continued)* provides an argument for care over how religion is presented, not for excluding it. It would probably be considered fatuous to suggest banning the teaching of science or of scientific method because, historically, science has been used for evil as well as good.

V. The Justification for Compulsory Education of Children Generally and for Including Any Specific Compulsory Elements in the Syllabus

It has been claimed that the concept of compulsory education by statute for all children anywhere in the world was first introduced in Scotland in 1494.[44] Although this was not initially enforced effectively, with encouragement by the post-Reformation church, a system of parish schools was early established. In England, by contrast, there was a deeply ingrained suspicion of education for the poor as likely to provoke unrest. However, during the eighteenth and nineteenth centuries, the growth of schools provided by dissenters and Roman Catholics spurred the established Church of England to add to those it already ran in some parishes.[45] These new church schools were largely initiated by the Church of England, through the British and Foreign Bible Society and the National Society.[46] The Elementary Education Act 1870 provided for local authority school boards to fill the gaps where there were no church schools, but the voluntary principle was still recognised. The state and the church between them had the duty to provide basic universal education but not to enforce it.

Including a place for religion in state schools in a modern pluralist society is contentious. There may be a reluctance to impose views on others, even on the part of those who firmly believe that their views are right. This may simply be a matter of personal temperament or it may reflect sympathy with classical liberal theories, which would limit the enforcement of acceptable behaviour in the private sphere.[47] What may be overlooked, however, is that, in practice, liberals are happy to use the law to enforce their beliefs on others when it suits them. An example is their readiness to compel children to attend school in the first place.

Therefore, before considering more fully the justification for including religious education and worship as an aspect of British schooling, it is appropriate to question to what extent compulsory schooling of children is justified at all. Classical liberal theorists have taken for granted that the rights of children are significantly different from those of adults and in particular that children should be denied the

---

[44] G.S. Osborne, *Scottish and English Schools: A Comparative Survey of the past Fifty Years* (London, Longmans, 1966), 5.

[45] Freedom for dissenters and Roman Catholics to teach was effected by 1791.

[46] The full name of the National Society was The National Society for Promoting the Education of the Poor in the Principles of the Established Church. This body (at www.natsoc.org.uk) still provides an important central resource for Christian schools in England.

[47] These may be distinct from a relativist refusal to recognise absolute moral standards.

choice not to be educated.[48] Education may be justified partly on the pragmatic ground that, unless individuals are equipped to make rational choices, they will be unable to know what they really want. Also, they will be unable to appreciate the principle fundamental to the preservation of public order that other individuals should equally be entitled to exercise a free choice over how they live their lives.

It is therefore taken as self-evident in a liberal society that the state should not only make education available for all children but should compel them to pursue it. However, this leaves open the ages between which education should be enforced and also the extent to which particular subjects in the curriculum or further detail in individual syllabuses should be prescribed.

Thus setting a legal age for making free choices is inevitably somewhat arbitrary. It is noteworthy that, in an increasingly complex society, the age of majority should nevertheless have been reduced to eighteen from twenty-one,[49] but the compulsory school leaving age remains at sixteen.[50]

If the education system as a whole is seen as essentially a means for enforcing objectively determined public benefits, the choice for the age at which compulsory education finishes could be justified in terms of social control. On this view, a longer compulsory education may be seen as a valuable means of keeping potentially aggressive young people out of trouble, both in their own interests and those of society.[51]

However, if the system is seen as primarily intended to enable young people themselves to live fulfilled and socially worthwhile lives, compulsion at an older age is more problematic. Taking this approach, it could be argued that the compulsory school leaving age should be lowered. The liberties of older children who did not want to stay at school would be respected and the finite economic resources that can be invested in skilled teachers could then be directed more effectively at those children who made clear that they wanted more education.[52]

---

[48] J.S. Mill, *On Liberty* (London, J.W. Parker, 1859), ch. 1: 'We are not speaking of children, or of young persons below the age which the law may fix as that of manhood or womanhood. Those who are still in a state to require being taken care of by others must be protected against their own actions as well as against external injury.'

[49] Family Law Reform Act 1969, s. 1.

[50] Education Act 1996, s. 8.

[51] On a more cynical view of modern 'spin-doctored' politics a high compulsory school-leaving age could be justified on the basis of excluding the young and untrained from the unemployment statistics.

[52] By contrast with schools, tertiary education is more obviously concerned with enabling those young people who opt for further or higher education. However, government does use forms of social control, other than legal coercion, to encourage larger numbers to study at the tertiary level.

If the emphasis in the education system is on enforcement, the system may concentrate on imposing predetermined patterns of socially desirable behaviour and belief and on equipping young people to do jobs other people consider to be socially useful. By contrast, if the emphasis is on enablement, the system is more likely to be directed at ensuring that pupils develop and fulfil their own potential as they choose.

Whatever the upper age for compulsory schooling, the older the pupil, the less justification there would seem to be for prescribing detailed curricula, let alone syllabus content. However, at a younger age, the issues are rather different. A politically liberal approach may justify the imposition of a wide curriculum on all children to ensure that they acquire enough basic knowledge and skills to build on as they choose when they are mature enough to make their own decisions. Providing choice for individual children in younger age groups, or rather for their parents, is difficult in practice, not least because schools are relatively small. Therefore, the curriculum at primary school level tends to allow few or no options. Even so, although such an approach may appear to represent an enforcement model, it is really concerned with enablement of individuals when they reach an age to exercise their own liberties.

Here, the English national curriculum is interesting in the manner in which it grades subjects, allowing greater choice to specialise as children grow older.[53] Thus the 'core subjects' are limited to mathematics, English and science.[54] By contrast, schools are also required to provide 'foundation subjects', such as history, geography, art and music,[55] but here pupils have a larger measure of choice even at an early stage. Significantly, these subjects may involve a considerable level of subjectivity, both in the choice of topics offered and in the manner in which they are presented. Here the liberal justification for compulsion is more vulnerable. However, if education is assessed in terms of the manner in which it develops critical awareness and judgement, forcing every child to study at least some of the foundation subjects may be considered essential.

Whether people, including children, should be compelled to accept certain benefits in life or should be left free to claim or reject them is a far from straightforward issue. Nevertheless, from a Christian perspective, an awareness of the reality of sin suggests that there is little ground for objection to making schooling for children compulsory and for

---

[53] The difficulty of balancing breadth of education with specialisation in depth and choice of preferred subjects is illustrated by a perennial debate over the best form of public examinations in schools. Thus the pattern of a small number of specialist Advanced Level subjects, usually two or three, has been changed for the 1999 sixth-form intake in England and Wales to a larger number, normally five, in the first year of the sixth form. Of these, two or three may be dropped in the final year.

[54] Education Act 1996, 354 (1).

[55] Ibid. s. 354 (2).

inculcating both an extensive body of knowledge and a wide range of skills. Because of sin, people often reject what would generally be regarded as beneficial both for themselves and for society as a whole. Even those who do not accept any concept of original sin are bound to recognise that the tendency to reject long-term benefits for short-term gratification is greater in children who have not yet acquired the information to make informed decisions or acquired the experience to understand and control their natural urges.

Christian attitudes to a compulsory curriculum and syllabuses are, however, likely to vary considerably. Some Christians may make common cause with those of an extreme materialist persuasion. The core subjects of mathematics, English and science prescribed under English law are of practical utility and can be presented in a relatively objective manner.[56] Other subjects are likely to be more subjective, both in the matter chosen to be taught and in the manner of presentation. Both the extreme materialist and some Christians may be afraid that such subjects are likely to influence children ideologically in a manner of which they disapprove and so would prefer these subjects not to be taught or for syllabuses to be restricted in such a manner as to exclude contentious material. On this approach, religious education would be a prime candidate for exclusion.[57]

By contrast, liberal humanists and other Christians with a broader perspective may be less worried about children being subjected to influences of which they disapprove, and more concerned that they should be introduced to as wide a body of knowledge as possible and be trained to exercise their own discrimination. For these, it may seem entirely appropriate for all schools to be required to teach the foundation subjects stipulated in the English National Curriculum and for all children to be required to study a broad selection of them. For such Christians, because religion, and specifically Christianity, are of paramount importance, all children should be assured the benefit of some exposure to them.

In practice, the attitudes to what should be taught in schools, of parents and others, whether they are Christians or not, will vary greatly, depending on personal experience and on the confidence placed in the teaching in particular schools. Generally, however, if the state education system is seen primarily in terms of enabling children and their parents to achieve what they consider the best education, the aim will be to maximise flexibility and choice. Schools will be required to teach the fullest range of subjects

[56] Both English literature and aspects of science may, however, be taught in controversial ways. A teacher's choice of English texts may greatly colour a pupil's perspective on life, and the battle between 'creationists' and 'Darwinian evolutionists' over the manner of the creation of the natural universe demonstrates an ideological conflict in the field of science.

[57] Thus religion is excluded from state schools in the USA under the doctrine of the separation of church and state.

possible. On the other hand, children, or their parents, will be given as much opportunity as possible to choose which subjects to study.

On such a view, the National Curriculum may be too restrictive in the range of subjects it requires schools to offer and too prescriptive in the subjects it requires individual pupils to study. On the other hand, religious education is in a legal category of its own. Schools are specifically required to provide it, but parents have a right to withdraw their children at any age and syllabuses are devised locally and in a manner designed to take account of what those affected believe should be covered.

VI. Religious Education

Particularly as this is an area where Christians have different perceptions of what is right, it should be made clear that I believe that religion should not be separated from other more material areas of life. In particular, this chapter is written in the conviction that it would be misguided to remove the legal framework that provides for a spiritual dimension in school life and the promotion of a religious ethos. Such a spiritual dimension may exist in community schools as well as in religious schools and the law serves to protect it in such cases. It must, however, be recognised that, particularly at secondary level, a genuinely Christian ethos is on any view much rarer in either type of school than would have been the case immediately after the coming into force of the Education Act 1944.

Against this background, there are Christians who would seek to reinforce the role of Christianity nationally by using the law to enforce a Christian ethos in all state schools. There are others who fear that the state system has become so secular and syncretistic that it would be better to exclude any provision for religion at all, at least in schools not explicitly religious. A significant proportion of Christians might be content to see religious education offered as an optional subject at secondary level, but would prefer it to be excluded otherwise. In the English and Welsh system, if religious education were no longer prescribed as part of the basic curriculum, it would be likely to disappear from non-confessional primary schools, except as a possible extra-curricular activity where the head teacher or governors allowed it.

Imposing an ethos on families who do not want it is likely to be counter-productive, and also questionable from a biblical perspective. Such an approach illustrates the problems associated with an enforcement model of the law. Any imposition of a religious ethos in all schools would probably provoke a reaction, with demands for secularisation. That may be seen, for example, as the cause of the 'laicisation' of the French state school system at the beginning of the twentieth century.[58]

---

[58] See Owen Chadwick, *A History of the Popes, 1830–1914* (Oxford, Clarendon Press, 1998).

By comparison, it may be said that the English and Welsh school systems have avoided such polarisation, because, since the nineteenth century, they have not so much sought to enforce religion on individuals through schools but rather to enable pupils in searching for a spiritual dimension within the school system. Today this is done in a flexible and varied manner with much scope for those out of sympathy to opt out altogether, whether they are secular and opposed to religion as such or are, for example, committed biblical Christians who are unhappy with the approach to religious education in a particular school.

Under the Education Act 1944 there was a duty on schools in England and Wales to provide 'religious instruction'. Instruction was the term used in non-confessional as well as in confessional schools, although it was stipulated that in schools not of a religious character it should not 'include any catechism or formulary which is distinctive of a particular religious denomination'.[59] By the Education Reform Act 1988, instruction was changed to 'education' and the ban on any catechism or formulary in non-denominational schools was amended so as to make clear that 'this is not to be taken as prohibiting provision in [an agreed] syllabus for the study of such catechisms or formularies'.[60]

The principle of including religion in the basic curriculum enables Christianity and religious and spiritual matters to have an airing they would be in danger of losing without legal support. A parallel may be drawn with the study of classical Latin and Greek languages and culture. These were seen for centuries as the staple of any form of advanced education in Britain, as in the rest of Europe. Historically, they were the background for the political and philosophical development of European culture from the Renaissance through to the nineteenth century. Yet they are not now part of the core curriculum and, despite much excellent and innovative teaching, have virtually ceased to be taught in state schools.

For the liberal humanist at the beginning of the twenty-first century, the study of religion may resemble the study of the Classics. It may be an interesting and intellectually stimulating subject but it is no longer of central importance. It might be desirable for both the Classics and religion to be guaranteed resources so that those wishing to study them may do so, but their role would be peripheral.[61] For a Christian, this approach may be either too much or too little. For some, because religion is often likely to be taught by teachers who do not believe it, it should be excluded altogether. For others, religion is fundamental in a way that no

---

[59] Education Act 1944, s. 26.
[60] See now the School Standards and Framework Act 1998, Sched. 19, para. 2 (5).
[61] On one view this 'free market' approach could be applied to all subjects. Whether they sank or swam would depend simply on whether enough parents or children opted for them.

other subject is and so should be guaranteed a special place such as it does at present have. From this perspective, even a diluted form of religious education can make pupils aware of the most important truths and there is therefore a Christian evangelical duty to promote at least the present legal position. Without it, children from non-religious homes would be denied the opportunity they have at present of learning something about basic religious belief at school. Those from religious homes could be more inclined to see their faith as simply a minority interest of their parents with no public relevance, which they might or might not feel like taking up for themselves

On this view, making some provision for the study of religion in the basic curriculum would seem to be a necessary means of ensuring that children are introduced to spiritual issues. There have been suggestions by secularists that religion should be replaced by lessons on humanist morality and civic virtue. However, even if today's society is regarded as overwhelmingly secular, the dominant part of the educational establishment in England seems to accept at present that a place for religious education can be justified as an important cultural topic introduced in an objective manner.[62] The wording of the present legislation envisages that religious studies is to be a genuine academic subject rather than a vehicle for imposing any specific belief system on children. In particular, formularies such as creeds, the Thirty-nine Articles and the Westminster Confession may be taught without a fear that they will be used by teachers as instruments for indoctrination.

It is significant to bear in mind that the restriction on education 'by means of any catechism or formulary' was included in the Education Act 1944 because of nonconformist fears that syllabuses could be used to inculcate specifically Anglican or Roman Catholic doctrines. This suspicion is less justified where creeds and formularies are presented as literary or historical texts which must be read and understood so that they may be judged critically by informed pupils, rather than learnt unquestioningly by rote.[63]

The problem remains that teaching is bound to be selective. A teacher may seem to promote, or indeed attack, a particular approach simply by spending time on it rather than on another.[64] Similarly, if one or two

---

[62] Hull, 'Religious Education', 32; Brenda Watson, *Education and Belief* (Oxford, Basil Blackwell, 1987), ch. 8, 'The Educational Case for Religious Education'.

[63] See Brian Gates (ed.), *Freedom and Authority in Religions and Religious Education* (London, Cassell, 1996), esp. ch. 10, John Hull, 'Freedom and Authority in Religious Education'.

[64] A parallel area of controversy during 1999 and 2000 has been the dispute over whether the Local Government Act 1988, s. 28, should be repealed. This provides that a local authority shall not 'intentionally promote homosexuality or publish material with the intention of promoting homosexuality'. The

minority faiths are given substantial treatment in a local agreed syllabus this may suggest that they are more important than others and, therefore, there may be a temptation to require all to be given equal but superficial, boring treatment that serves only to inoculate pupils against religion generally. This problem is not peculiar to religious studies. Especially in arts subjects, such as literature and history, the choice of syllabus and the texts studied within the syllabus inevitably give particular emphases. However, the problem can be reduced by allowing full discussion over content, by providing diversity so as to ensure a genuine basis for comparison, and by building in choice wherever possible.

The law for English schools enables Christians to take part in an ongoing dialogue both with other faiths and with secular interests over the content of agreed syllabuses and the manner in which they are taught in particular schools.[65] Rather than enforcing any particular faith position, the law is designed to enable both society and individual children to find their own. Part of the tension here is that religion is more than just a subject in the curriculum. It provides an ethos that may pervade an institution. The legislation on schools recognises such pervasive elements in the whole curriculum of a school by requiring that it should be 'a balanced and broadly based curriculum which (a) promotes the spiritual, moral, cultural, mental and physical development of pupils at the school and of society'. The more mundane and materialist aim is put second, that it '(b) prepares pupils at the school for the opportunities, responsibilities and experiences of adult life'.[66]

For some, general aspirations of this sort are meaningless. They are far too vague to be enforced and are banal even as a test for expressing the general aims of the institution.[67] It is like saying 'our aim is to do good'. Nevertheless, the formula can serve as an encouragement. It brings to mind the words of Philippians 3:8, that 'whatever is true, whatever is pure, whatever is lovely, whatever is admirable – if anything is excellent or praiseworthy – think about those things'. To this extent, although it is

---

[61] *(continued)* wording contrasts with the approach of the Education Act 1944 in censoring religious creeds and formularies. A restriction on promoting homosexuality would seem to be comparable to a restriction on promoting a particular faith or, say, atheism. The Local Government Act 1988 clearly does not prohibit homosexuality being discussed but it appears to make some teachers feel vulnerable if the topic is covered, rather as a ban on promoting Islam or Judaism might make teachers nervous of discussing those faiths at all in class.

[65] See further J.D.C. Harte, 'The Religious Dimension of the Education Reform Act 1988' (1989) 1 *Ecclesiastical Law Journal* (5)32.

[66] Education Act 1996, s. 351 (1).

[67] J.D.C. Harte, 'Worship and Religious Education under the Education Reform Act 1988 – a Lawyer's View' (1991) 13 *British Journal of Religious Education* 152.

not explicitly Christian, such a formula gives continuing encouragement for Christian values and provides a rallying point for those of good will who seek to maintain the coherence of society. It contradicts the postmodernist assumption that there are no objective values and the materialist assertion that the spiritual is an illusion. However, those of a secular frame of mind may object that moral principles directed at respect for one's neighbours are as much humanist as religious. The Christian or the committed member of another faith will want more.

The difficulty is highlighted by one of the few court cases concerned with religion in schools: *R v Secretary of State for Education ex p R and D*.[68] There, McCulloch J refused to intervene when parents of two primary school children in Manchester challenged a school for failing to meet the statutory requirements for adequately Christ-centred religious education. The judge was able to sidestep the issue because the children concerned had changed school by the time of the hearing. Nevertheless, it was apparent that the problem had been an integrated syllabus that made it difficult to locate coverage of Christian stories and teaching.

From a Christian perspective there is a significant problem if a school is pervaded by an anti-religious ethos where teachers denigrate religious views and values, for example in respect of sexual morality. Even at a material level, a relativist approach, which denies any overarching objective values, may undermine a child's capacity to appreciate beauty and harmony in either the created order or in the arts. This will make it more difficult for children to sense the awe of God's providence in creation or to develop an understanding of the purpose for human creativity, let alone a sense of human sin and the need for redemption.

Although parents may withdraw their children from religious education and from unacceptable teaching on sexuality[69] it is obviously impracticable to monitor the entire syllabus. Conversely, the legal provision for a specific niche for religious education provides a focus for ensuring that children are given a sound and adequate presentation of Christianity. Where this is achieved, there may be some hope of pupils being equipped with insight to see inconsistencies elsewhere, for example if a history teacher runs down the church or a biology teacher represents religion as obscurantist.

VII. The Place of Christianity Within Statutory Religious Education

Local agreed syllabuses for those schools not explicitly confessional 'shall reflect the fact that the religious traditions in Great Britain are in the main Christian whilst taking account of the teaching and practices of the other

---

[68] Unreported, CO/2202/92, 26 February 1993.
[69] Education Act 1996, s. 405.

principal religions represented in Great Britain'.[70] Non-confessional schools constitute both the largest number of schools and cater for some three-quarters of all pupils. As confessional secondary schools are rare in most parts of England and Wales, the agreed syllabuses are of strategic importance at secondary school level.

The specific religious education formula in England and Wales with its emphasis on Christianity, and the whole framework embedding religious education in the curriculum put the initiative back with Christian parents and teachers. The law can not be used as a crude means of imposing Christian orthodoxy. Rather, it invites reasoned debate in local authority syllabus committees, and among governors and teachers. It offers an instrument to help concerned Christian parents to have their views listened to. Neither the law nor agreed syllabuses can ensure that children encounter the living Christ. However, if the legal framework is used effectively, such an encounter can be made more likely.

Recognising the diversity of modern British culture and the aspirations of citizens from minority faiths the syllabuses are intended to promote understanding between different cultural groups in a mixed society. Whether it is linked to racial and cultural identity[71] or is simply a matter of considered personal conviction, their religion is likely to be of immense importance to individual members of a faith. It is therefore vital for others to have some understanding of their neighbour's faith if offence is to be avoided. From a Christian perspective, laws that promote racial tolerance and harmony are commendable and children should be offered insight into the faith of others.

However, agreed syllabuses must first 'reflect the fact that the religious traditions of Great Britain are in the main Christian'. In terms of social order and mutual respect it is indisputable that Christianity has been a fundamental element in the evolution of British culture and its political institutions. On a purely pragmatic level, as the historic religion of the host culture, it is sensible for Christianity to be emphasised. There is much scope for argument over what proportion of the population today see themselves as 'Christian'. However, considerably more people would classify themselves as Christian, rather than as belonging to any alternative faith.

Therefore, if education is expected to provide children with understanding of the society in which they live, the statutory formula for agreed syllabuses of religious education would appear to be both sensitive and realistic. Nevertheless, the meaning of the formula that requires syllabuses to reflect the fact that the 'religious traditions of Great Britain are in the main Christian' is notoriously difficult to tie down. It has been suggested that the formula implies that a certain proportion of every syllabus

---

[70] Education Act 1996, s. 375 (3).
[71] Cf. *Mandla v Dowell Lee* [1983] 2 AC 548 and *Ojutiku and Oburuni v Manpower Services Commission* [1982] IRL 418.

should relate to Christianity, and certainly at least 50 per cent, or that Christianity must be given at least as much treatment as other 'principal religions'. It can be argued that the formula at least means that Christianity should be taught at every level at a school.

In practice, if a syllabus conference agrees a syllabus and this is given effect by the local education authority as complying with the statutory formula,[72] it is unlikely that the syllabus will be condemned by a court either on the ground that it is too explicitly Christian or that it is not sufficiently so. On the normal *Wednesbury* principle it would have to be framed in a manner no reasonable authority properly advised on the law could endorse.[73] Provided the syllabus allows significant treatment to Christianity and does not give greater weight to any other faith, it will be difficult to argue that the formula has been breached.

On the other hand, so long as recognition is given to the range of minority faiths now practised in Great Britain, a local agreed syllabus that provides for a sound and extensive introduction to the Christian faith will comply with the Act. It is therefore crucial for Christian parents, teachers and churches to use the machinery for ensuring that syllabuses have an explicitly Christian content, and in particular that they enable children to be introduced to the Jesus of the New Testament by reading the Bible itself.

The safeguard here is the requirement that there must be unanimity among the subcommittees represented on a conference. Each group has a single vote,[74] so a majority within a group is sufficient. Christians on the local authority and teachers' committees could be outvoted. However, on the general faith committee, the members appointed are to represent 'such Christian denominations and other religions and denominations of such religions as, in the opinion of the authority, will appropriately reflect the principal religious traditions in [the] area'.[75] Further, the numbers appointed 'shall so far as is consistent with the efficient discharge of the committee's functions, reflect broadly the proportionate strength of that denomination or religion in the area'.[76] The local education authority, therefore, must give a majority of places to Christian representatives where Christians are in a majority in the area.

A further safeguard to ensure proper representation requires the local education authority to 'take all reasonable steps to assure themselves that [a person they select] is representative of the religion [or denomination] in question'.[77] Failure to take such steps could result in a syllabus being invalid.[78] Finally, the committee representing the Church of England

---

[72] Education Act 1996, Sched. 31, para. 10.
[73] *Associated Provincial Picture Houses* v *Wednesbury Corporation* [1948] 1 KB 223.
[74] Education Act 1996, Sched. 31, para. 6.
[75] *Ibid.* para. 4 (2) (a).
[76] *Ibid.* para. 4 (4).
[77] *Ibid.* para. 7 (1).
[78] *Ibid.* para. 7 (2).

clearly has a veto over an unsatisfactory syllabus. The choice of its representatives must in practice be approved by the diocese. Although these representatives could hold beliefs Christian parents were unhappy about they are, in practice, likely at least to guarantee a substantial place for Christianity in the syllabus. If it is considered that the contribution of such representatives could be improved, Christians working through the synodical system of the Church of England have the means to influence or replace them.

In a particular school, even a syllabus with excellent Christian content may be taught in an off-putting or downright cynical manner that parodies the faith it is intended to present. In such circumstances, individual Christian parents must make a judgement if the religious education in their children's school is so bad that the children should be withdrawn. There is a view that if children are told about the Christian faith by teachers who lack a personal faith in Christ they may be inoculated against the real thing, and these fears must be taken seriously. However, a good teacher who is not a believer can nevertheless make religion interesting, like any other subject, and may present beliefs in a balanced manner that leaves children free to make their own decision as to their truth.[79] Even a modest introduction to Christianity at school can provide a framework of vocabulary and basic concepts to prevent churches and Christians seeming impenetrable, alien or intimidating.

Inoculation against faith may be a danger as a result of boring presentation or what appears to be inconsistent behaviour on the part of a teacher who professes to be a believer. On that basis, however, children may be inoculated against Christianity through regular attendance at church just as much as through religious education classes in school. The point here is that if the education system is seen in terms of enablement rather than enforcement, the legal framework for religious education in English and Welsh schools allows for Christianity to be presented in a valid manner in ordinary state schools, which can provide a bridge into Christian fellowship and into the church, especially for children with no regular Christian contacts.

Satisfactory Christian teaching in schools will be achieved only if Christian parents and teachers and other Christians are involved as governors or otherwise in arguing for resources to be allocated to religious education and for it to be taught in an interesting, committed manner. A major explanation for many of the complaints about the vague and unconvincing teaching of the subject in some schools may be that, because of lack of resources for specialist teachers who are committed, it is given to teachers with no interest in it and who are either too busy already or may even be kept from teaching other subjects because of their unsuitability as teachers.

[79] Phil. 1:15.

VIII. Worship

If the legal provision for religious education in English and Welsh schools is looked at askance by some Christians, the further requirement of daily worship in English and Welsh schools provokes at least equal controversy.[80] Now tucked away in Schedule 20 to the School Standards and Framework Act 1998, is the crucial detail, again originating in the Education Reform Act 1988, on the form of worship in non-confessional schools. This requires collective worship to be 'wholly or mainly of a broadly Christian character'.[81] Collective worship is defined as of a broadly Christian character 'if it reflects the broad traditions of Christian belief without being distinctive of any particular Christian denomination'. Not every act of collective worship in the school need comply with this definition, however, 'provided that taking any school term as a whole, most such acts which take place in the school' do comply.

As with religious education, the complex wording on worship reflects a hard-fought compromise in which pressure groups obtained a measure of entrenchment for Christianity.[82] Again, there is dissatisfaction from Christians with opposing views. Those who seek to preserve Christian worship in schools fear that the wording is still broad enough to allow for multifaith or non-Christian acts of worship, which they consider wrong. By contrast, some Christians consider that, because of the present materialist character of society, acts of worship in ordinary schools are a travesty and should cease altogether.

There is a deeply ingrained view within the educational establishment, notably among specialists in religious education, that if worship is to be treated as an aspect of religious education children should be encouraged to be critical and to stand outside what is presented.[83] This appears to militate against it serving as an expression of living faith by teachers and pupils. An alternative view is that worship is fundamentally different from religious education and should provide a genuine channel for contact with God. It is here that the enforcement of worship as an element in the normal school day is most likely to be criticised. Criticism of school worship comes both from secularists who resent what they see as indoctrination and from some Christians who fear that the result will be hypocrisy on the part of staff forced to participate against their own lack of belief, and also alienation of children forced to take part in something which they find meaningless.

[80] School Standards and Framework Act 1998, s. 70.
[81] *Ibid.* Sched. 20, para. 3 (2), subject to para. 4.
[82] See n. 11 above.
[83] See generally Brenda Watson, *Education and Belief* (Oxford, Basil Blackwell, 1987), ch. 14, 'Assembly and Worship in School'.

A key point here is the nature of the rights of teachers[84] on the one hand and of parents[85] on the other. Each group may avail themselves of conscience clauses and may opt out from participation in religious education or worship or both. As religious education tends to be seen more readily, simply, as one academic subject among others, the opting out provisions are particularly important with regard to worship. It may be argued, here, especially, that both teachers and children may be under pressure to conform, which makes the right to opt out illusory. Teachers may fear covert discrimination in being overlooked for promotion. Children may be fearful of seeming the odd one out. These arguments are significant, but they may be used simply as secularist excuses for depriving families of the choice of maintaining a religious dimension to school life, or they may be an expression of insecurity by teachers over their own uncertain beliefs.

The anti-discrimination provisions to protect teachers are very explicit. Under the School Standards and Framework Act 1998, s. 59, no one shall be disqualified as a teacher in a non-confessional school 'by reason of his religious opinions, or of his attending or omitting to attend religious worship'.[86] Neither are teachers to be required to give religious education against their will,[87] and there is to be no reduction in remuneration or disadvantage in promotion by reason of the teacher not giving religious education or 'by reason of his religious opinions or of his attending or omitting to attend religious worship'.[88]

If the legal provisions for worship in schools are seen as essentially enabling, it should be possible for those committed to maintaining it to support those teachers who do not wish to take part and to ensure that adequate resources are provided to make the worship effective, including participation in leading worship by those with appropriate gifts, such as local clergy.

So far as parents and children are concerned, parents may withdraw children from religious education or worship at any state school, including those that are specifically religious. Furthermore, parents have a right to

---

[84] School Standards and Framework Act 1998 ss. 59 and 60.
[85] *Ibid.* s. 71.
[86] *Ibid.* s. 59 (2).
[87] *Ibid.* s. 59 (3).
[88] *Ibid.* s. 59 (4). In religious voluntary controlled or foundation schools, religious considerations may only be taken into account in respect of reserved teachers appointed specifically to teach religion. They may be taken into account in respect of teachers generally in voluntary aided schools. (*Ibid.* s. 60). However, no discrimination is allowed on religious grounds in any state school in respect of non-teaching staff (*ibid.* ss. 59 (2) (b) and 60 (3)). In a religious school, therefore, a groundsman or cleaner may not be disqualified by reason of their religious opinions or because of attending or omitting to attend religious worship.

send a child, for such periods of time as are reasonably necessary, for alternative religious education somewhere else, in sessions at the beginning or end of school.[89] The fear of a child feeling an odd one out may be more difficult to allay than the fear of discrimination on the part of a teacher. However, it would be drastic to deprive the majority of children of an important aspect of school life to avoid any risk to the sensitivities of a minority who are in any event allowed to opt out.

For the Christian, worship is a fundamental part of daily life and it is therefore desirable for the law to provide a framework within which it may be freely practised both on a weekly day of rest and in the context of the working day.[90] In particular, it is desirable that children should have the opportunity to learn within such a framework. However, unsatisfactory school worship, as much as the absence of any spiritual framework in a school, is an important matter for concern. If the education system is seen in enforcement terms, imposing worship led by indifferent unbelievers on a resisting body of children may well seem a travesty.

If school worship is seen in terms of enabling children to gain insight into a fundamental dimension of human life, it will be important to ensure that schools provide appropriate worship, particularly for the benefit of those children who will have no opportunity to experience it otherwise. The questions then arise as to what is appropriate worship and whether it can effectively be provided for in the ordinary English school today.

It is significant here that the statutory safeguards on choice in school worship go further than individual rights for parents to withdraw their children. In a non-confessional school the arrangements for worship are determined by the head teacher after consultation with the governors.[91] Variations may be made to the normal provisions for collective worship. In particular, the Christian emphasis may be varied by the head teacher to take account of '(a) any circumstances relating to the family background of the pupils which are relevant for determining the character of the collective worship which is appropriate in their cases, and (b) their ages and aptitudes'.[92]

More radically, in a non-confessional school, if requested by the head teacher, the SACRE may determine that the normal Christian emphasis in collective worship shall not apply at all. This power cannot be used to authorise worship distinctive of any Christian or other religious denomination, but it may allow for worship to be distinctive of a non-Christian faith.[93] Thus, in a predominately Muslim area, a community school may

---

[89] *Ibid.* s. 71.
[90] Pss. 61:8; 86:3; 88:9; Acts 2:46; 17:11.
[91] School Standards and Framework Act 1998, Sched. 20, para. 4. In a religious school, they are determined by the governors after consultation with the head teacher.
[92] *Ibid.* para. 3 (5) and (6).
[93] *Ibid.* para. 4.

be authorised to hold daily worship in the form of Muslim prayers. However, Christian children may then be withdrawn and there would seem to be no reason why alternative worship should not be provided for them at the beginning or end of the school day, for example at a nearby church. The legislation, therefore, does provide a framework within which children may be enabled to experience regular weekday worship without imposing a burden on those whose parents do not want them to enjoy that opportunity.

There are logistical difficulties for head teachers in providing satisfactory daily worship in schools, although the practical problem would seem to have been considerably reduced in that the school day is no longer required to start with worship, and worship may be arranged 'for all pupils or ... for pupils in different age groups or in different school groups'.[94] In practice, worship takes place during assemblies that provide an opportunity to express the communal entity of the school. If there is no hall large enough to accommodate the entire school at one time, assemblies may still be valuable to promote the cohesion of year groups. However, pupils may not even have a daily assembly of this sort. On a daily basis, even if there is no larger assembly, pupils will normally have to gather for a short time for administrative chores and notices. If worship is associated in a perfunctory manner with such chores the present law may be counter-productive.

On the face of it, the statutory formula could allow for children to be grouped for religious education according to their chosen faith and for the worship to be associated with the relevant faith. Administratively, if all classes had religious education during the same period, such an arrangement would seem perfectly feasible and there would seem no reason why the agreed syllabuses for religious education should not provide options for children from different faiths. The objection to such an expedient would doubtless be that it would be divisive. It may be questioned whether that needs to be the case. If all children are able to learn about their own religion, or about such religions as they choose, and are encouraged to respect the fact that other pupils in the same school come from different traditions, the idea of religion may appear more interesting and thought provoking.

Arguments have been advanced, not least by Christian teachers, that, rather than a daily act of worship, it would be better if the law provided for occasional but more substantial acts of worship, such as a weekly service, well planned to demonstrate the relevance and attractiveness of religion, and specifically of Christianity. This could be particularly appropriate in secondary schools and it would, in any event, seem possible without changing the law.

It may be that an adequate legal framework for ensuring that non-confessional schools enabled their pupils to experience appropriate

---

[94] *Ibid.* para. 2 (2).

worship could merely stipulate that schools must make facilities available for services to be held on a regular basis by local churches or other religious bodies. On the other hand, if it is desirable for worship to be provided in schools, the present law does allow considerable flexibility for developing a variety of patterns, whereas attempts to modify it could result in worship being eliminated altogether from the majority of state schools. Ordinary state schools can still provide a Christian ethos for children in an area where there are no specifically religious schools, and the general statutory requirement for collective worship strengthens the position of those seeking to maintain and to develop community schools of that type.

The different considerations that arise in secondary schools by contrast with primary schools are particularly relevant for collective worship. By this stage, children may have become more cynical and dismissive of religion but, provided there is support from staff for worship in an appropriate modern form, it may be particularly valuable to demonstrate that worship is possible and can be meaningful for adolescents. Where there is commitment by staff, parents and governors, many primary schools at any rate continue to show that school worship is possible and valued. If children in secondary schools react against worship, rather than accepting the abolition of the statutory requirement, it may be that churches need to rethink radically what worship really is and what form it should take in contemporary society.

An underlying problem in respect of worship in schools is differing approaches among Christians over the nature of worship and over the forms Christians may appropriately support or take part in. The requirement that collective worship in schools should not be distinctive of any Christian denomination suggests that worship in a school is something different from worship in a church. Clearly, any sacramental form of worship would be ruled out by the legal formula in any event. Some will take the view that school assemblies with a required element described as 'worship' are acceptable and important to retain if they express the worth of the moral and cultural contribution of Christianity and of other faiths with readings and music. However, there is a feeling held by many, including a proportion of Christians, that school worship in non-confessional schools must not be more explicit, for fear of putting unwilling pupils in the position of addressing a deity in whom they do not believe.

Similarly, Christians are bound to be worried if school worship is used as an occasion for praying or making obeisance to anything other than the One God. However, linguistically, worship may be pitched at many different levels, from adoration and devotion in words and ceremonies, to expressions of honour and respect. At this more modest level, a school assembly can provide a valuable spiritual dimension to the school day if it includes uplifting readings, prayers and music consistent with Christian belief but that would not be offensive nor appear to be seeking to proselytise the secular agnostic or the child from another faith. At this level, school worship can be an important part of the educational experience, which will help children to understand the claims of religion and enable them to accept those claims for themselves.[95]

Worship literally implies affirming the worth of that which is worshipped. For the believer it will entail praise and prayer that presuppose the existence of the being worshipped. However, the non-believer who takes a child to visit a cathedral, or to listen to BBC sung evensong or a hymn by George Herbert presumably considers each experience worthwhile and is unlikely to admit that they amount to indoctrination. It is difficult to see why the unbeliever should consider school worship that is not overtly evangelistic as inherently any more dangerous, in principle, unless he or she is desperately trying to resist God's call to faith. Such worship may well be limited from a Christian point of view, but it may still be valuable in enabling children from homes where there is no church association to be touched by Christ. It can also lay a rich deposit that can be drawn on if it is brought alive later in life.

The limited case law on this subject emphasises the modest nature of the legal requirement for daily school worship. In *R* v *Secretary of State for Education ex parte R and D*, McCullough J endorsed the view of the Secretary of State that collective worship 'must in some sense reflect something special or separate from ordinary school activities [and be] concerned with reverence or veneration paid to a power or being regarded as supernatural or divine, and that the pupil, at his or her level, should be capable of perceiving this'. The reference to worship of a Christian character did mean that some 'special status' had to be accorded to the person of Jesus, but not necessarily more than that.[96] From the perspective of the Christian believer such a concept of worship may seem anaemic. However, it is a minimum requirement, not a norm. Once again, what the law does at this point is to provide an opportunity for involved Christians to ensure that something much more vibrant and recognisably Christian is provided wherever possible.

---

[95] The enactment of stories from sacred writings are a special case here. The nativity story is the obvious example and it would seem a sad impoverishment of the British primary school if this were banished. However, it may be that such plays should not be seen as worship but as drama. On that basis, also, the enactment of stories from other faiths may be less problematic for the Christian. Indeed, set forms of worship are, objectively, art, in the form of literature, music and drama. On that basis it may often be possible to take part in them in a school setting without commitment to them, as where religious music is sung during a concert.

[96] *R* v *Secretary of State for Education, ex parte R and D*, unreported, CO/2202/92, 26 February 1993.

It is argued, therefore, that the statutory provisions for worship in schools in England and Wales do not need to be considered as objectionable, either by the secular observer or by the Christian or by the member of another faith. The law is essentially enabling rather than coercive. It safeguards the rights of children from a religious home to be taught in an environment sensitive to what the religious person will consider the most important dimension of life, and makes possible the experience of worship by all children. The law cannot compel living worship, but it is sufficiently flexible to allow for it and to encourage diversity so that children are not bored or alienated from the gospel. It allows but does not compel an ordinary state school to develop a recognisably Christian ethos.[97]

IX. The Church and the Place of Denominational Schools

A community without worship is essentially a secular community. Even in a heavily secular culture, some geographically based communities still have a Christian identity, related to one or more local church congregations. In other cases, a gathered congregation of believers forms a distinct community of believers within the wider secular society. There may be schools serving secular communities that want their children to be educated in a secular ethos. In many schools the secular ethos may be so deeply ingrained that Christians are bound to be chary of worship as a sham. There may also be a suspicion held by some Christians that school worship is likely to be dominated by suspect religious ideas found in parts of most denominations.[98] Nevertheless, my view is that it is difficult to justify changing the law by removing the general provisions on religion in schools, so depriving children in ordinary local state schools of the opportunity to be educated in a spiritually living environment where that is still attainable. In any event, the legal requirements for worship in non-confessional schools should not be sacrificed until adequate provision has been made nationally for religious schools.

Where there are differences between Christians over the suitability of particular legal rules, it is sometimes right for one party to submit to restriction rather than claim a liberty others may find frightening or believe to be damaging.[99] However, where each believes the views of the other to be potentially harmful, particularly to Christian children and to the integrity of the gospel, as it is perceived by non-believers, there is a

---

[97] Examples of materials available for Christian worship in any state school are available from the National Society (at www.churchschools.co.uk).
[98] Such a division of feeling was strongly expressed when the paper on which this chapter is based was discussed at the academic conference of the Lawyers' Christian Fellowship.
[99] 1 Cor. 6:12 and 10:23.

considerable dilemma. Ultimately, this may be resolved by prayerfully submitting the matter to God and by allowing him to create a common mind. However, in the meantime, the history of Christianity since the Reformation, and particularly during the twentieth century, has demonstrated that God's answer may be that of diversity, with mutual respect and a sharing of what is held in common, despite deeply held differences.[100]

In the context of religion in ordinary state schools in England and Wales, the law provides a measure of flexibility in both the teaching of religion as an academic subject and in common worship. This should allow local education authorities and the people belonging to individual community schools to work out satisfactory solutions that suit their particular circumstances. Individuals who are unhappy with the solution, whether teachers or parents, are entitled to opt out. The law may therefore contain considerable diversity and may also allow for the possibility of future development, for example as the religious complexion of those connected with a school changes.

In many areas in England and Wales, especially at secondary level, the only school available will be a community school. Therefore, if that school is truly to represent the community, there is a considerable opportunity and a sobering responsibility laid upon Christian teachers and parents and on local churches to take a more active role in ensuring that worship is worthy of God, but also that it takes into account different religious sensitivities. There is a similar responsibility for Christians to play a role in influencing the content and quality of local education authority agreed syllabuses.

In some areas, however, church schools offer a vital alternative to non-confessional community schools. It is important to note here that Church of England schools have a different underlying policy from other confessional schools. As a national church, the Church of England has a statutory responsibility for schooling generally and not only in respect of church schools. Under the Diocesan Boards of Education Measure 1991, every diocese is required to have a Diocesan Board of Education answerable to the diocesan synod.[101] The functions of the Board include a responsibility generally '(a) to promote or assist in the promotion of education in the diocese, being education which is consistent with the faith and practice of the Church of England' and '(b) to promote or assist in the promotion of religious education and religious worship in schools in the diocese' as well as specifically '(c) to promote or assist in the promotion of church schools in the diocese and to advise the governors of such schools and trustees of church educational endowments and any

---

[100] The great high-priestly prayer of Jesus in John 17:11 particularly underlines the essential aim of Christian unity and the difficulty of relating it to an agreed understanding of truth.

[101] Diocesan Boards of Education Measure 1991, s. 1.

other body or person concerned on any matter affecting church schools in the diocese'. Further, there is a duty '(d) to promote cooperation between the Board and bodies or persons concerned in any respect with education in the diocese'.[102]

The Church of England sees its responsibility for specifically denominational schools as providing a Christian ethos for all families who want it and not just for those who are members of the denomination.[103] Thus admissions policies may give priority to regular church attenders but a child who attends a local Methodist or United Reformed church on a weekly basis may be more likely to obtain a place than one who goes to the local Anglican parish church once a month or so.[104]

In an increasingly materialist society, it may be that religious communities will become increasingly estranged from state provision in areas where belief and the integrity of a religious life view are threatened. In such conditions the present network of church schools, both Church of England and Roman Catholic, is likely to become more important for Christian parents. The Church of England perception of its schools as open to all who seek a Christian ethos for their children is particularly apt from an evangelical Christian perspective. It enables children to encounter the gospel and its practical outworking, unselfconsciously and in a secure environment. Particularly if non-religious schools become more definitely secular, the Church of England offers a framework for all Christians and for those of other faiths to expand the provision of schools that have a spiritual dimension and that take religion seriously. The present Labour government has indicated that it welcomes new church schools, and the Church of England has taken the initiative in exploring the potential by setting up the Archbishops' Council Church Schools Review Group, chaired by Lord Dearing. The report by Lord Dearing's Group has suggested an immediate initial target of two new Church of England church schools in each of the forty-two dioceses.[105]

One of the major features of the Church of England as a national church is that it sees its mission in parochial terms, providing a Christian presence, with centres for worship, pastoral care and teaching, within every community and with responsibility for every square metre of ground. Many church schools originated as parish schools. A vision for today may be that every parish should have a primary school with a specific link to the local church and that every adolescent should have access to a secondary school with a positive Christian framework. In

---

[102] *Ibid.* s. 2.
[103] Commission on Religious Educations in Schools, *The Fourth R: The Durham Report on Religious Education* (London, SPCK, 1970).
[104] Admissions arrangements for state schools are generally provided for in the School Standards and Framework Act 1998, Part III.
[105] Archbishops' Council Church School Review Group: *The Way Ahead* (London, Church House Publishing, 2001).

some cases this may mean new Church of England aided schools. In others it may mean the diocese assuming a new responsibility for particular community schools. In other cases it may mean new Christian foundation schools set up on ecumenical lines in parallel with local ecumenical partnerships. These partnerships provide a framework where Church of England parishes and worship centres are shared with other denominations, demonstrating a practical Christian unity. Where non-confessional schools have succeeded in maintaining a Christian ethos, the legislation has ensured that they are non-denominational. More positively, such schools set a precedent for future ecumenical cooperation.

X. Conclusion

There is a distinction between ensuring that Christians and other religious people are able to bring their children up in a religiously sympathetic school environment and providing that all children should be exposed to a spiritual dimension in school, unless they or their parents choose to opt out. The first approach seems to be consistent with thinking on human rights[106] and would be satisfied by adequate provision of confessional schools throughout the country. If the state is neutral it should provide equal financial support for both secular and religious schools.

However, this chapter has argued that, from a Christian perspective, the existing arrangements for religious education and worship in English and Welsh non-religious state schools are consistent with a wider view of the law. These arrangements, for all their limitations, offer a means of enabling not only children from Christian homes but children from all backgrounds to fulfil their potential as human beings made in the image of God, by making them aware of a spiritual dimension to life and by offering them the possibility of an informed choice of a religious basis for their own future lives.

Such legal arrangements must be treated with sensitivity, since there is always a danger that they may be perceived as a system for enforcing one set of cultural values at the expense of others. Even though Christians may be convinced that biblical values are true, enforcing them may be politically counter-productive and also inconsistent with the concept of God, whose grace is freely given and that needs to be freely accepted through genuine faith. The suggestion of this chapter is that a primacy for Christianity should be sought, unashamedly, but on the basis of adjusting to the claims of other faiths and of secularists for separate or

---

[106] The Human Rights Act 1998 and the European Convention on Human Rights underline this trend. The specific rights to religious freedom in the context of education depend upon Article 9 of the Convention and Protocol 1, Article 2.

supplementary representation of their positions. This can be justified in secular terms because of the historical importance of Christianity in British culture.

Some Christians are sceptical or deeply distrustful of Christianity being taught, and even more of worship being provided, in state schools, unless those schools are specifically confessional. Nevertheless, it has been argued here that Christians should not be browbeaten into accepting the downgrading in schools of Christianity, let alone all religion, on the grounds that it is necessary for reasons of cultural diversity or civil liberty.

Here democratic machinery is important for determining the place of religion, and specifically of Christianity, in schools. Secular democracy and the popular consensus it seeks to express are neutral from a Christian perspective. They need not be seen as relativist concepts that undermine the role of Christianity in society. Rather, they may serve as a dynamic means for establishing the real nature and level of commitment in society. They are assumed as authoritative by modern secular society. They may, therefore, be enlisted to stimulate and make more effective the possibility of revival feeding back into school life.

Thus the manner in which change may be democratically determined by the choice of individual school communities is an important issue. Notably, this includes the election of governors, and, more widely, elections to such bodies as the councils that constitute local education authorities. Also important here are elections to diocesan synods that oversee Church of England representatives on syllabus committees and on local authority SACREs.

The elaborate arrangements of English local syllabus committees and SACREs constitute a sophisticated model for adjusting religious provision in state schools to suit local conditions. Such complex legal arrangements may be necessary if law is to be used as an effective system for enabling good ends. Thus a voluntary controlled school in England or Wales may opt for aided status. By contrast, it must be accepted that a community school in an area with a large number of children from other faiths may obtain the approval of the SACRE to opt out of the normal pattern of religion dominated by Christianity.

Christians from different theological traditions and with different personal experiences may be more or less optimistic about the value of the English Law on religion in schools as a means of advancing Christ's kingdom. Thus, despite the provisions for opting out from worship, some may take the view that worship should be abolished in non-confessional schools because children from non-Christian homes will be wrongly induced to take part in something that, for them, is not genuine. However, if this view were followed through it would make questionable the whole idea of public Christian worship attended by unbelievers or, for example, broadcast on television. It would throw in doubt the practice of children unsympathetic to church being taken there by their parents.

True Christian worship presupposes a genuine involvement on the part of the worshipper. However, even committed Christians may take part in a particular act of Christian worship without engaging their faith. Others, who are not committed, may nevertheless take part at various levels of understanding and involvement. The New Testament envisages non-believers being present at worship and being converted by the experience.[107]

In a school context, collective worship in non-confessional schools would seem the most contentious aspect of the present law on religion in schools. The case of Christian opponents of school worship becomes stronger the more often worship is poorly conducted by teachers with no personal commitment. From a Christian perspective there is certainly an immense responsibility if the existing law is retained to ensure that those who lead school worship are committed to it and to pray for committed Christian teachers with appropriate gifts to be called to use the opportunity.

Within close proximity Jesus is recorded as saying on the one hand, 'He who is not with me is against me',[108] and 'He who is not against you is for you'.[109] Jesus' contrasting words underline the fact that, in Christian terms, ultimately, no situation can be entirely neutral. However, there is danger in Christians obstructing a venture with which they are not entirely happy, but that may turn out to accord with God's will. This danger is greater than seeking to make the most of a system that, despite the defects inevitable in any human institution, professes to advance Christian values.

The argument of this chapter is that where law is seen as coercive and is used to enforce values its role should be strictly confined. However, where it is used as a means of enabling or empowering the individual to attain a fuller life, and in particular to have access to the truth of the Christian gospel, law may properly serve a wider function. If the law providing for a religious element in schools in England and Wales is seen as enabling rather than enforcing Christian values, the propriety of retaining that element is compelling. If it becomes clear that society has become overwhelmingly antithetical to the Christian faith, furthering Christ's kingdom may point to Christians concentrating on the development of an increasing number of specifically Christian schools within the state system, spread across the country. In the meanwhile, the present law has value in supporting the retention of a Christian ethos, especially in those non-confessional schools where there are committed Christian teachers.

---

[107] Acts 14:23–25. Rather less obvious but also relevant is the experience of those who take part in worship without clearly understanding what they are doing. Starting from their muddled or misguided understanding God may reveal the truth to them (e.g. Acts 17:23).

[108] Luke 11:23; cf. Matt. 12:30 and Mark 9:40.

[109] Luke 9:50

3

The Contracting Society: A Misplaced Faith

Ewan McKendrick

I. Introduction

In his Foreword to *Christian Perspectives on Law Reform* Lord Mackay of Clashfern stated that 'sadly perhaps, the civil legislator cannot ignore the realities of the human condition, however far from the ideal it may be'.[1] Rules of law must be formulated so that they can be applied in the world as it is. The legislator must face up to the practical problems that confront people in today's society and seek to find workable solutions to them. In seeking to resolve these problems it is not always possible to impose by law solutions consistent with Christian principles, because Christian values cannot invariably be transplanted into an increasingly secular, pluralist world. This is not to deny the importance of defending Christian values or of seeking to persuade others of their value; it simply recognises that many people in our society have rejected them and that it may often be inappropriate to *impose* them by way of law.

This gulf between an increasingly secular, regulated society on the one hand and Christian principles and values on the other presents us with a number of difficulties when seeking to analyse modern law from a Christian perspective. Two difficulties can be highlighted at the outset. The first is pragmatic and flows from the sheer volume of legislation produced by the modern regulatory state, much of which is difficult, if not impossible, to analyse from a Christian viewpoint. The general principles the law adopts and the policies it pursues may be analysed from a Christian perspective, but the detailed rules often cannot be analysed in this way. Health and safety at work and environmental law may provide two good examples here. It is possible to construct a Christian perspective on the issues, values and policies that underpin or should underpin health and safety at work or environmental law as a whole[2] but this perspective does not yield answers to the mass of detailed questions that arise in each area of law (e.g. as to acceptable noise levels at work, the level of

---

[1] Paul R. Beaumont (ed.), *Christian Perspectives on Law Reform* (Carlisle, Paternoster, 1998).

[2] See, for example, D. Harte, 'A Christian Approach to Environmental Law?' in Beaumont, *Christian Perspectives on Law Reform*, 51.

acceptable emissions, and the regulation of the way in which we should dispose of chemical substances). The second difficulty is one of principle. The fact that the gulf between Christian principles and the values of society is gradually widening creates an issue for Christians as to how far they should go in terms of seeking to halt the drift away from Christian values and principles.[3] To what extent is it legitimate to seek to resist any attempt by society to depart from legal principles based on Christian principles and, further, to what extent is it appropriate to seek to go further and endeavour to re-establish Christian principles that have been lost by society at some time in the past? Of course Christians, along with every other member of society, have the democratic right to seek to persuade others of the validity of their views, but the question in my mind is one that relates to the wisdom of seeking to use the law in order to bring about conformity with Christian values.

The aim of this chapter is not to offer a Christian perspective of the law of contract, in the sense of some idealised conception of contract law that is fully consistent with Christian principles and values. Rather, it is to suggest that there is no such thing as a distinctively Christian law of contract, albeit that there are Christian values which, it can be argued, either do underpin or should underpin the law of contract.[4] Further, it is argued that in many respects the law of contract wrestles with problems that arise because of our imperfect or fallen nature and, to some extent, the law inevitably reflects these imperfections. Finally, the chapter ends with something of a puzzle, namely the renewed emphasis being placed by policy-makers on 'contractual' thinking, albeit that the 'contracts' so created do not create the usual rights and liabilities that flow from the creation of the traditional, legally binding contract. It is in this sense that we live in what might be termed a 'contracting society', albeit that the 'contracts' so created are unlikely to do the work hoped of them in terms of solving the problems society currently faces.

II. Two Distinctions

Before moving on to the substance of the essay, it is necessary to make two preliminary points, which both involve the drawing of distinctions. The first is that a distinction must in my view be drawn between conduct or actions contrary to God's law and those that should be regarded as unlawful by the law of the land. Adultery provides a good example. There is no doubt that adultery is a violation of God's law for

---

[3] These issues are helpfully explored in more detail by John Stott in his essay 'Pluralism: Should we Impose our Views?' in *idem, Issues Facing Christians Today* (Basingstoke, Marshalls, 1984), 45.

[4] An example of a principle that underpins the law of contract and is consistent with Christian values is the maxim *pacta sunt servanda*.

humankind,[5] but today few would argue that it should constitute a criminal offence.[6] Sometimes conduct violates both God's law and the law of the land; murder is an obvious example in this category. But where should we draw the line between conduct that violates both God's law and the law of the land and that which violates God's law but does not, or should not necessarily infringe the law of the land? In many ways Christians are on safer ground when they claim that particular forms of conduct violate God's law. They expose themselves to much greater criticism when they argue that a violation of Christian principles should simultaneously constitute a crime or a civil wrong.[7]

The second point is that a distinction needs to be drawn between principles that should be applied by a Christian when entering into a contract and the rules of contract law that should apply to all in society, whether Christians or not. More is expected of a Christian who is seeking to live his or her life in accordance with biblical standards than is required by the law of the land. In many ways the most difficult problems arise where Christians enter into contracts, not on their own behalf, but as employees, perhaps senior employees, of a secular organisation, such as a multinational corporation. A conflict of loyalty may then arise between the standards that regulate the Christian in his or her personal life and the standards accepted and operated by the company itself.[8]

III. Is There Such a Thing as a Distinctively Christian Law of Contract?

The claim that there is no such thing as a distinctively Christian law of contract is based on two arguments. The first is that there is no obvious answer, from a Christian perspective, to many of the problems that currently confront the law of contract.[9] For example, which types of breach of contract should entitle the innocent party to terminate further performance of the contract? This issue has proved to be one of some controversy in the light of the enactment of section 15A of the Sale of Goods Act 1979, which restricts the right of a commercial buyer to terminate a contract of sale on the ground that the seller has breached one of the implied conditions contained in sections 13–15 of the Sale of

---

[5] Exod. 20:14.
[6] It may of course have private law consequences. Thus it may be relevant in divorce proceedings.
[7] This is not to imply that Christians should never argue that a violation of God's law should also constitute a violation of the law of the land. It simply points out that the one does not automatically follow from the other.
[8] The ways in which this conflict can be resolved or minimised are beyond the scope of this chapter.
[9] This point is not, of course, confined to the law of contract (see p. 71 above).

Goods Act 1979. Some commentators have welcomed the reform on the ground that it gives the courts greater flexibility and should produce fairer results, while others have criticised the change in the law on the ground that it gives rise to too much uncertainty in an area where there is a definite value in having clear rules.[10] As far as I am aware there is no answer to this issue that can claim to be distinctively Christian.[11] These examples could be multiplied. Suppose two parties enter into a long-term contract and the deal has turned out to be a bad bargain for one of the parties, to the extent that it is no longer economic for that party to continue with performance. Should the courts have the power to adjust or terminate the contract on the ground that performance has become impracticable? Courts in America[12] and in some European jurisdictions have such a power and may well exercise it, but English courts enjoy no such absolving power.[13] Or suppose that a party enters into a contract as a result of a misrepresentation made to him by the other party to the contract, or that she enters into the contract while labouring under a mistake that has not been induced by the other party to the contract?

Should a party who has been induced to enter into a contract by a misrepresentation made by the other party always be entitled to set aside the contract? At first glance, the answer might appear to be 'yes', but what about the case where the misrepresentation is made innocently and causes no loss to the person to whom the misrepresentation is made? To allow the latter party to rely on the misrepresentation in order to extricate herself from the contract is to permit the misrepresentation to act as an 'excuse' in order to enable a party to get out of what has turned out to be a bad bargain.[14] More difficult is the case where the mistake has not been induced by the other party to the contract. Every legal system has had to struggle with the question of whether, and to what extent, a mistake should entitle a party to set aside a contract and the matter is little closer to

---

[10] See, for example, G.H. Treitel, *The Law of Contract* (London, Sweet & Maxwell, 10th ed., 1999), 744–745.

[11] In many ways the answer to the question is to be found in the balance to be struck between the value of certainty, on the one hand, and 'fairness' or 'justice' on the other.

[12] See, for example, *Aluminium Company of America v Essex Group Inc* 499 F Supp 53 (1980), discussed more generally in Digwa-Singh, 'The Application of Commercial Impracticability under Article 2-615 of the Uniform Commercial Code', in E. McKendrick (ed.), *Force Majeure and Frustration of Contract* (London, Lloyds, 2nd ed., 1995), 305.

[13] *Davis Contractors Ltd v Fareham Urban District Council* [1956] AC 696, discussed below, p. 79.

[14] For this reason an English court might use its discretionary power under section 2 (2) of the Misrepresentation Act 1967 to relegate the misrepresentee to an action in damages: see, for example, *William Sindall plc v Cambridgeshire County Council* [1994] 1 WLR 1016.

definitive resolution today than it was in Roman times.[15] The invocation of Christian principles is unlikely to produce an instant solution to this intractable problem.

The fact that there is no obvious answer, from a Christian perspective, to a number of the difficult issues that face the law of contract lends weight to the second argument in support of the proposition that there is no such thing as a distinctively Christian law of contract, namely that contractual thinking is simply not central to the Christian gospel.[16] For example, it is difficult to believe that contractual principles were at the heart of the thinking of members of the church in early New Testament history. In Acts chapter 2 we are told that 'the believers ... had everything in common. Selling their possessions and goods, they gave to anyone as he had need.'[17] We have here a picture of a vibrant, sharing, loving community, which, given the daily increase in numbers,[18] was obviously attractive to others. It is manifestly not a picture of autonomous individuals asserting their rights against each other.[19] Similarly, when the apostle Paul instructed the Ephesian church about the characteristics that should be evident in the relationship between husband and wife, parent and child, and master and slave he prefaced his remarks by stating, 'Submit to one another out of reverence for Christ.'[20] The focus is on what you can give to a relationship, not what you get out of it. The emphasis is on love, trust, giving and sharing, not on self-interest and rights.

Yet it would be wrong to conclude from this that the Bible has nothing to say about contracts. If we replace the word 'contract' with 'covenant' it

---

[15] The fact that it continues to give rise to difficulties in the English courts can be seen from the recent case of *Clarion Ltd* v *National Provident Institution* [2000] 2 All ER 265.

[16] Two points are being made here. The first is that rule making and compliance with the rules is not central to the Christian gospel in the sense that 'no-one is justified before God by the law' (Gal. 3:11; although as Paul elsewhere makes clear this does not imply that Christians are given a licence to ignore the law). The second point is that, to the extent that 'contractual thinking' can be equated with autonomous individuals asserting their rights against each other and doing only what they are required to do and no more, it does not correspond with the emphasis placed in the New Testament passages cited in the text.

[17] Acts 2: 44–45.

[18] Acts 2:47.

[19] Of course it can be argued that the law of contract is not necessarily about the assertion of rights and the defence of autonomy. A more cooperative model of the law of contract can be constructed, but I doubt whether even the most cooperative model of the law of contract would accurately reflect the practices of Christians as described in Acts 2. See further pp. 86–91 below.

[20] Eph. 5:21.

becomes apparent that the Bible has a great deal to say on the subject: the existence of a covenant between God and his people runs throughout both Old and New Testament.[21] It is of course true that the nature of the covenant changes radically between Old and New Testament, but the evidence to support the centrality of covenant thinking is clear. Shining through these covenants we find pictures of God's faithfulness,[22] his love and our inability to discharge our own covenant responsibilities. Perhaps here we can find values that should inform our law of contract, namely the importance of fidelity to our obligations, both in relation to our obligations to God and our obligations to our fellow human beings.

While fidelity to our obligations is an important value in the law of contract and in our society, it is not an absolute value, and for good reason. Two examples will suffice to show why fidelity to our obligations is not an absolute value. First, suppose that two contracting parties enter into a contract under which one party gives to the other permission to use his music hall for a series of concerts. After the conclusion of the contract, but before the time set for the first concert, the music hall is destroyed by a fire that started accidentally. Is the owner of the music hall liable to the other party for a failure to make the music hall available as promised? He has failed to honour his obligation to make the music hall available for the concerts as he promised he would. But it seems unfair to hold him liable because he could not have foreseen that the concert hall would be destroyed by an event beyond his control. An English court would undoubtedly absolve the owner of the music hall from any liability in such circumstances.[23] Secondly, suppose that a twenty-year-old employee enters into a contract with his employer under which he agrees to work for that employer for the rest of his life and he covenants that he will not, under any circumstances, work for anyone else. A modern court would have no difficulty in striking down such an agreement on the ground that it is in restraint of trade.[24] In this case the importance of fidelity to the employee's promise is outweighed by arguments based on the need to preserve the autonomy and future freedom of the employee.[25]

Why then do we not elevate fidelity to our promises to an absolute value? If God can keep his promises absolutely, why can we not do so as

---

[21] See, for example, Exod. 34:10 ff.; Hebrews 8–9.

[22] On which see the valuable chapter by T.G. Watkin, 'The Concept of Commitment in Law and Legal Science', in P. Beaumont (ed.), *Christian Perspectives on Human Rights and Legal Philosophy* (Carlisle, Paternoster, 1998).

[23] This example is based on the well-known English case of *Taylor* v *Caldwell* (1863) 3 B & S 826, in which it was held that the contract between the parties was frustrated because the destruction of the music hall rendered performance of the contract impossible.

[24] *Horwood* v *Millar's Timber and Trading Co* [1917] 3 KB 305.

[25] See S.A. Smith, 'Future Freedom and Freedom of Contract' (1996) 59 *Modern Law Review* 167.

well and demand that others do so? One has only to ask the question to realise the answer: we are simply unable to keep our promises all of the time. And this is the nub of the issue. The law of contract must wrestle with us as we are, with all of our imperfections, and, to some extent at least, it must reflect these imperfections. Indeed, many of the difficulties the law of contract encounters arise from the fact that it is seeking to regulate or deal with the consequences of our imperfect nature. We cannot see into the future or, perhaps more accurately, our ability to do so is limited. We break our promises from time to time (some more often than others) and, consequently, the trust we are willing to repose in others has its limits. The fact that we are not omniscient, that we often pursue our own self-interest, and that our willingness or ability to trust each other is limited all feature at numerous points in the law of contract. The concern that the law of contract has with these three issues is worth further brief exploration in the following three sections below, before seeking to draw some threads together.

IV. We Are Not Omniscient

The fact that we are not omniscient is an obvious point to make. Perhaps not so obvious is the point that our cognitive limitations go some way towards explaining the content of some of the rules of the law of contract.[26] These cognitive limitations apply both to the judges and to the contracting parties themselves.

Take first the case of the judges. Judges who hear cases must seek to ascertain who is telling the truth, and they cannot look into the minds of the parties in order to decide where truth actually lies. As is well known, English contract law takes an objective approach when deciding whether or not two parties have concluded a contract.[27] A good example is provided by the case of *Centrovincial Estates plc* v *Merchant Investors Association*.[28] The claimants let premises to the defendants at a yearly rent of £68,320, subject to review from 25 December 1982. The parties were obliged by their contract to endeavour to reach agreement before 25 December 1982 on the then current market rental value of the property and to certify the amount of the current market rental value. In June 1982 the claimants wrote to the defendants inviting them to agree that the current rental value should be £65,000. The defendants accepted this invitation. When the claimants received the defendants' written acceptance they immediately contacted the defendants to inform them that

---

[26] See, for example, M. Eisenberg, 'The Limits of Cognition and the Limits of Contract' (1995) 47 *Stanford Law Review* 211.
[27] See, for example, the judgment of Blackburn J in *Smith* v *Hughes* (1871) LR 6 QB 597.
[28] [1983] Com LR 158.

they had meant to propose £126,000 and not £65,000. The defendants refused to agree to this new figure and insisted that a contract had been concluded at a rental value of £65,000. The claimants sought a declaration that no legally binding agreement had been entered into between the parties. The Court of Appeal refused to grant such a declaration, holding that the parties had entered into a contract at a rental value of £65,000. The defendants neither knew nor reasonably could have known that the claimants had made a mistake when formulating their offer.[29]

The justification for the adoption of an objective approach to the question of whether or not the parties have reached agreement is both pragmatic and commercial, namely that great uncertainty would be caused if a person who appeared to have agreed to certain terms could escape liability by claiming that she had no 'real' intention to agree to them. What is the Christian response to a case such as *Centrovincial*? The answer is not at all clear. On the one hand it can be argued that the case was wrongly decided on the ground that the claimants never intended to propose a figure of £65,000.[30] On the other hand, the defendants were found to be unaware of the mistake the claimants had made and it can be argued that the claimants should take responsibility for their own mistakes. If we had judges who had perfect knowledge they could perhaps apply a subjective test of agreement[31] but, in the absence of such knowledge, English law has committed itself to an objective test,[32] despite the fact that the consequence of doing so may be to impose on one of the parties an agreement to which he did not in truth consent.[33]

---

[29] This finding might seem rather surprising given that the rental value stated by the claimants had actually gone down, but the court accepted that the defendants did not know that a mistake had been made.

[30] The case has been criticised on rather different grounds by P.S. Atiyah, 'The Hannah Blumenthal and Classical Contract Law' (1986) 102 *Law Quarterly Review* 363.

[31] It is, however, possible to adopt a subjective test of agreement, even in the absence of perfect knowledge. Some legal systems, such as South Africa's, have tended towards the adoption of a subjective approach. The difficulty with a subjective approach is that the judge cannot look into the mind of the contracting parties, and so must seek to infer what was going on in their minds by the outward appearance, which inevitably turns attention to more objective factors.

[32] There are of course different varieties of objectivity, on which see generally W. Howarth, 'The Meaning of Objectivity in Contract' (1984) 100 *Law Quarterly Review* 265.

[33] Any disadvantage in this respect is outweighed by the measure of certainty provided by the objective standard. The need for certainty in commercial transactions is an important factor when seeking to explain the result and the reasoning in *Centrovincial*.

Turning now to the contracting parties themselves, cognitive limitations can be seen to apply with equal force here and they have a significant role to play in terms of explaining some of the rules that make up the law of contract. For example, contracting parties must plan for the future, but the future is, to a large extent, unknown and one party may mispredict a future turn of events. In *Davis Contractors Ltd v Fareham UDC*[34] the claimants agreed to build 78 houses for the defendants for £94,000. The work was scheduled to last for 8 months but, owing to shortages of skilled labour, the work took an extra 14 months to complete and cost £115,000. The claimants, in an attempt to recover a sum of money in excess of the contract price, argued that the contract had been frustrated. The House of Lords concluded that the contract had not been frustrated so that the claimants could not escape from the bad bargain into which they had entered. The decision that the claimants were confined to the terms of the original contract may seem a harsh one but, had the decision gone the other way, it would have created a new principle of uncertain ambit and given some hope to a party who wished to extricate himself from a bad bargain. Instead, the House of Lords established a clear rule that sends out a plain signal to contracting parties to the effect that the courts will not lend their assistance to a party looking for a way out of what has turned out to be a bad bargain.[35] The decision has been criticised on the ground that it adopts an unduly restrictive approach to the scope of the doctrine of frustration. But, given that the parties know that the future is uncertain and that they can insert into the contract a variety of clauses designed to minimise or reduce that uncertainty,[36] the decision in *Davis Contractors* seems to me to be a defensible one.

Once again, this is an issue on which reasonable minds can disagree. Some will focus on the hardship caused to the party called upon to perform what has, through no fault of his own, become an excessively onerous contract. On the other hand, others will point to the uncertainty that would be caused by the mere existence of a power in the court to adjust a bad bargain and they would also argue that such uncertainty can be exploited by a party who has entered into a losing bargain in order to extract a concession or an adjustment from the other party to the contract. This does not seem to be a case where there is a distinctively Christian solution or one that will be accepted by all Christians. The Bible simply does not tell us what should happen when a contracting party incorrectly predicts the future course of events or the future direction of a particular market and suffers substantial losses as a result.

Cognitive limitations also apply to attempts to control risk. Take the case of a carrier who knows that every so often goods that have been entrusted to her company will be lost or damaged as a result of the

---

[34] [1956] AC 696.
[35] *The Nema* [1982] AC 724, 752 per Lord Roskill.
[36] Such as *force majeure* clauses and hardship clauses.

carelessness of one of her employees. She takes all possible steps to reduce the possibility of loss, but knows that she cannot eliminate the risk entirely. The goods carried by her company vary enormously in value. Her fear is that one day goods of high value will be lost and that the loss will have to be borne by the company, to her possible financial ruin. So her lawyers suggest that she draft an exclusion clause or a limitation clause to provide her with some protection against the consequences of the carelessness of her employees. It is easy to take a dim view of exclusion clauses on the ground that they serve to take away the rights of the weak and the vulnerable. While there is undoubtedly an element of truth in this view,[37] it must also be said that both exclusion and limitation clauses perform a useful function in terms of allocating the risk of the occurrence of certain events.[38] The law must seek to strike a balance and recognise that exclusion and limitation clauses perform useful functions as well as functions that are deemed to be socially undesirable.[39]

This balancing exercise is made more difficult by the fact that the future is unknown and that the parties are, at the time of entry into the contract, seeking to allocate the risk of uncertain events. With the benefit of hindsight it can sometimes be seen that the risk of loss could have been more judiciously allocated by the parties, but the validity of a clause should not be tested with the benefit of hindsight. The validity must be tested at the moment of entry into the contract, when the risks are allocated by the parties.[40]

Is there a distinctively Christian approach to this balancing exercise? Probably not. Prior to the enactment of the Unfair Contract Terms Act 1977, there may well have been room for a Christian perspective on the ground that there was not much to be said for a party who broke his contract and excluded liability to the other contracting party without considering the interests of that other party. But the Act now requires that account be taken of the interests of the other party,[41] and the

---

[37] As evidenced by the enactment of the Unfair Contract Terms Act 1977 and the Unfair Terms in Consumer Contracts Regulations 1999 (SI No. 2083).

[38] In many cases the problem relates to the consequential economic loss suffered by the innocent party. Such losses can be both substantial and difficult to quantify. Many contracting parties are understandably reluctant to accept liability for these losses.

[39] Particularly where the effect of the exclusion clause is to leave the consumer with significant losses (the loss may be either physical or economic), but no means of redress.

[40] A fact recognised by section 11 (1) of the Unfair Contract Terms Act 1977, which states that the reasonableness test is to be applied at the time of entry into the contract, not the time at which the breach occurs.

[41] Either through declaring certain clauses to be invalid, for example, in sections 2 (1) and 6 (2) of the Act, or by subjecting them to a test of reasonableness, for example, in sections 2 (2), 3 and 6 (3) of the Act.

balancing exercise the Act requires the courts to carry out is not amenable to a dogmatic approach. Christian principles may, and should, influence the balancing exercise, but they do not dictate a particular outcome.

Given these uncertainties and our inability to eliminate them completely, there is a value in having a clear rule even though it can, on occasion, lead to harsh results. The virtue of a clear rule is that it enables the parties to know where they stand and to calculate the cost of their actions. The disadvantage of a clear rule is that it can periodically produce harsh results. The virtue of a flexible rule is that it can prevent such an injustice arising, but it does so at a cost. That cost is that the parties may not know where they stand, their lawyers may not be able to give them clear-cut advice and one party, usually the more powerful party, can then exploit that uncertainty to its advantage. The balance between certainty and flexibility is another of these balancing exercises where it is difficult, if not impossible, to be dogmatic. Much depends on the facts and circumstances of the individual case.

Two examples will illustrate the point. The first is the decision of the Privy Council in *Union Eagle Ltd* v *Golden Achievement Ltd*.[42] The claimant purchaser agreed to buy a flat in Hong Kong and paid 10 per cent of the purchase price (HK $420,000) as a deposit. The agreement specified the date, time and place of completion, and time was stated to be in every respect of the essence of the agreement. Completion was to take place on or before 30 September 1991 and before 5 p.m. on that day. Clause 12 of the agreement stated that, if the purchaser failed to comply with any of the terms and conditions of the agreement, the vendor had the right to rescind the contract and forfeit the deposit. The claimant failed to complete by the stipulated time and tendered the purchase price 10 minutes after the time for completion had passed. The vendors refused to accept late payment, rescinded the contract and forfeited the deposit. The claimant refused to accept the defendants' decision to rescind the contract and brought an action seeking to have the contract specifically enforced. Its attempt was unsuccessful.

Should the defendants have been entitled to terminate the contract and forfeit the deposit in such circumstances? Again, there does not appear to be an obvious answer to this question from a Christian perspective because, in a case such as this, the balance between certainty and flexibility is a difficult one to strike. The Privy Council in *Union Eagle* came down on the side of certainty. This approach can be criticised on the ground that it was excessively harsh on the purchaser who lost the opportunity to complete the purchase of the property as a result of being 10 minutes late in tendering the price. The 10-minute delay was

---

[42] [1997] AC 514, noted by J.D. Heydon, 'Equitable Aid to Purchasers in Breach of Time-Essential Conditions' (1997) 113 *Law Quarterly Review* 385; and J. Stevens, 'Having your Cake and Eating it? *Union Eagle Ltd* v *Golden Achievement Ltd*' (1998) 61 *Modern Law Review* 255.

unlikely to have caused significant harm to the vendor and, even if it did, such harm could have been made good by an award of damages. Why allow the vendor to terminate in such a case? The answer is that the purchaser was in breach of a clause stated to be of the essence of the contract. It, or its advisers, should have known that late tender of the price would give to the vendors the right to terminate the contract and forfeit the deposit. All that happened was that the courts enforced the contract the parties had made, and they declined to intervene and rewrite the contract in the name of 'fairness'.

In the view of Lord Hoffmann, giving the judgment of the Privy Council, the paramount consideration was that the parties should be able to know with certainty that the terms of their contract would be enforced. As he pointed out, a jurisdiction to intervene in cases of 'unconscionability' would not produce such certainty because contracting parties and their advisers would rarely be able to ascertain in advance of a court hearing whether or not the vendor was entitled to terminate. If a 10-minute delay was held not to be long enough, would an hour suffice? If not an hour, what about two hours, or a day? From the perspective of a vendor of land such uncertainty could be very costly because, pending the resolution of the issue, he would be unable to sell the land to another, willing purchaser. The land would effectively be frozen pending the outcome of the litigation. It can be argued that this approach gives too much weight to arguments from certainty. Further, the mere fact that a court has a jurisdiction to intervene does not mean that it is going to exercise it in any particular case. On the other hand, as Lord Hoffmann pointed out, the mere existence of a discretion to grant relief could be used as a negotiating tool by a defaulting purchaser and so would lead to the very uncertainty he was not prepared to countenance.

In my view the approach of the Privy Council in *Union Eagle* has much to commend it. It promotes certainty where certainty is required (in relation to the vendor's freedom to deal with its own land) but gives the courts some flexibility where the need for certainty is not so important. Certainty is not such an important commodity in relation to the financial consequences of termination, in particular the retention by the vendor of the deposit paid by the purchaser. And it is in the latter connection that Lord Hoffmann left open the possibility that a purchaser might be able to obtain relief in exceptional cases. In so far as the sum retained by the vendor exceeds a genuine pre-estimate of its loss or a reasonable deposit[43] the court has 'a discretion to order repayment of all or part of the retained money'.[44] And, where the vendor has been unjustly enriched by improvements made at the purchaser's expense, the purchaser may have a personal restitutionary claim to recover any unjust enrichment the

---

[43] On which see *Workers Trust & Merchant Bank Ltd* v *Dojap Investments Ltd* [1993] AC 573.
[44] [1997] AC 514, 520.

vendor has obtained as a result of the termination.[45] In other words, the effect of the decision is to restore to the vendor the 'freedom to deal with his land as he pleases',[46] but, at the same time, the vendor is not given the same freedom in relation to the financial consequences of termination. This accommodation of the conflicting interests of the vendor and purchaser seems to be a reasonable one, but it is not one that commands universal support, largely because the balance between certainty and flexibility is a difficult one to strike and different people will strike it in different places.

The second example is based on the facts of *Arcos Ltd* v *E A Ronaasen & Son*.[47] Suppose that a buyer enters into a contract with a seller under which the buyer agrees to buy a quantity of wood cut into lengths of 1 m each. The wood is cut in lengths that vary between 98 cm and 102 cm. The differences in length do not impair the utility of the wood to the buyer. The price of wood has dropped in the market so that the buyer now wishes to get out of the contract and buy the wood elsewhere. So he rejects the goods and terminates the contract. Is the buyer entitled to behave in this way? Until recently English law would, on the basis of the decision of the House of Lords in *Arcos*, have allowed the buyer to terminate. Today, as a result of the enactment of section 15A of the Sale of Goods Act 1979,[48] the answer is not so clear. It is no easy task to work out whether or not the buyer should be entitled to terminate in such a case. There is a very good reason for saying that he should not be entitled to do so because his reason for wishing to terminate is a 'bad' one in that it is collateral to the contract itself; he has acted in bad faith in order to get out of what has turned out to be a bad bargain. But the arguments are not all one way.

English law traditionally has not placed any emphasis on the motives of the party who is seeking to justify his decision to terminate the contract. The focus of the courts in the past has not been on the motives of the parties but on the existence or otherwise of an entitlement to terminate.[49] The virtue of this approach is that it does not require the courts and legal

---

[45] [1997] AC 514, 523.
[46] *Ibid.*
[47] [1933] AC 470.
[48] This section states that, where, for example, the consequences of a breach of section 13 of the Sale of Goods Act 1979 are so slight that it would be unreasonable for a commercial buyer to reject the goods, then he is to be confined to a remedy in damages.
[49] This is so to the extent that a party who puts forward no reason or a bad reason for terminating can still justify his decision to terminate if a good reason existed at the time of his decision to terminate, even if he was, at the time of termination, unaware of the existence of his right to terminate on this ground: see H. Beale, *Chitty on Contracts* (London, Sweet & Maxwell, 28th ed., 1999), para. 25-013.

advisers to inquire into or speculate about the motivations of the party who wishes to terminate. But the cost of it is that it can allow parties to terminate for what might be thought to be unfair reasons, as in *Arcos* itself. If we focus solely on the facts of *Arcos* itself, the case for concluding that the buyer should not be entitled to terminate the contract seems a strong one. But if we take a broader approach, and consider the signals the decision sends to the market, the answer may not be so clear. The seller was, after all, a contract breaker who had broken an important term of the contract. Should we seek to protect the contract breaker by requiring the buyer who wishes to terminate to show not only that the term broken was an important one but that the consequences of the breach were sufficiently serious to him? And, if the consequences of the breach must be sufficiently 'serious' before a buyer can terminate, how serious must 'serious' be? Here we can usefully return to the decision of the Privy Council in *Union Eagle* where emphasis was placed on the need to promote certainty in relation to the decision to terminate so that the parties can know where they stand in relation to their freedom to deal with the subject matter of the contract. Should the same approach also apply to contracts for the sale of goods? In a fast-moving market there is much to be said for clear rules so that buyers and sellers can know, with some certainty, the legal consequences of their actions and decisions.

Enough has been said to demonstrate that these issues are difficult and admit of no easy answer. The fact that we are unable to predict the future or to work out where exactly we should strike the balance between certainty and flexibility means that it is difficult to offer a distinct Christian perspective on these issues because Christians are no more able than the rest of the population to predict the future course of events in any detail, nor do they have any special insight as to where the balance between certainty and flexibility should be struck.

V. Our Pursuit of Self-Interest

To a greater or lesser extent all human beings pursue their own self-interest; this is the root of sin. The fact is that we do not live our lives as God intended us to live them.[50] This raises three issues of concern to this chapter. The first is that the law must face up to the fact that we all commit wrongs and devise appropriate means of redress. Much of the law of contract is concerned, not with contracts performed according to their terms, but with contracts that for one reason or another have gone wrong. The law of contract, at least as it appears in the books, is concerned largely with people who do not perform their contractual obligations, who exercise duress or undue influence over the other

---

[50] Again, this is not intended to imply that we should not strive to lead our lives as God intended us to live them. We should: see, for example, Phil. 3:12–15.

contracting party or who induce people to enter into contracts by telling them lies. From a Christian perspective, it is clear that such wrongdoing should not be encouraged but Christian principles do not appear to dictate a particular remedial outcome (e.g. whether the remedy granted should be termination of the contract, damages or specific performance).

Secondly, the fact that we are imperfect seems to place limits on what the law can legitimately demand of us. Take 1 Corinthians chapter 13 as an example. It ends with the famous words, 'And now these three remain: faith, hope and love. But the greatest of these is love.' Can these verses be used as the foundation for the recognition of a duty of good faith and fair dealing[51] or a more cooperative law of contract? At first sight, it may seem clear that they can be so used. But there is a need for caution here. The word Paul uses for love is *agape*. Unlike *eros*, *agape* does not imply a love for something worthy of love; it is a selfless love that extends to the love of those who are unworthy. What would *agape* love mean in practical terms for the law of contract? It would transform it completely because we would be 'obliged' to act in a selfless manner, over and above the terms of our contract. Should such an exacting standard be imposed as a matter of law? The answer must be 'no', because to do so would be to impose a standard with which we could not comply. As Dr Bruce Milne states, 'Agape-love is not difficult at all, it is impossible! It is impossible for fallen men and women consistently to love in the way that God loves us in Christ Jesus.'[52] Furthermore, the imposition of *agape*-love as a matter of law seems to be inconsistent with the very nature of such love. It is a love demonstrated not as a matter of compulsion but volition. It is a gift of God[53] to be exercised freely; it is not a man-made rule that demands adherence.

An example may illustrate the point. Suppose a householder enters into a contract with a woman who runs a business. The contract price is the market price for the job but, unknown to the householder, the woman is in desperate financial straits. She is a widow and is struggling to bring up her three children. Should the law of contract require the householder to offer the woman more by way of payment simply because she is a widow who finds herself, through no fault of her own, in difficult financial circumstances? In my view the answer has to be 'no'. Now assume the householder is a Christian. Perhaps he or she ought to do

---

[51] The point being made here is not that the law should not recognise a duty of good faith and fair dealing, nor that good faith must be equated with *agape* love. Rather, that it is not possible to translate *agape* love into the law of contract. Good faith has been chosen simply because it might be used by some as a vehicle for the translation of 1 Corinthians 13 into the law of contract.

[52] *We Belong Together* (Leicester, IVP, 1978), 42.

[53] As evidenced by the fact that 1 Corinthians 13 is located in the middle of Paul's exposition of the gifts of the Holy Spirit.

something to help her, but he or she should not be compelled by the law of contract to do so. Christians are exhorted to 'give proper recognition to those widows who are really in need'[54] and the outworking of *agape*-love in the life of an individual Christian may lead him or her to give a gift to the widow or otherwise offer her support, but that is different from being required by the law of contract to increase the price to some extent in order to help meet the widow's needs.[55]

This may seem rather negative in that it can be argued that it fails to recognise that the law can be used as a means of bringing out the good in us and discouraging the bad. This brings me to the third issue, which concerns the extent to which the law of contract should be used in an attempt to transform our human nature rather than simply reflect it. In other words, should the law of contract seek to encourage the good in us, or should it simply try to limit or prohibit the bad? English contract law is generally rather good at dealing with the bad in us. The doctrines of economic duress[56] and undue influence[57] have expanded in recent years in an attempt to regulate the types of pressure that can be applied when seeking to persuade a party to enter into a contract and to ensure, as far as possible, that the decision to enter into a contract is a free one, and not one dictated by a person upon whom the contracting party is unduly dependent. A contract induced by a misrepresentation can, in principle, be set aside, even when the misrepresentation is made innocently.[58]

While English law may be good at regulating the bad in us, it may not be quite so good on the positive side in terms of encouraging cooperation and altruism. Once again, an example may be helpful.[59] Suppose that a company knows that there is oil under a farmer's land. Using a middleman it approaches the farmer and bids for the land. It offers the market

---

[54] 1 Tim. 5:3. See further vv. 4–14.

[55] Any attempt by the law of contract to impose an obligation to increase the price in this way would run into numerous practical difficulties: how much should the householder be required to give to the widow? Should every householder who enters into a contract with the widow be required to offer her extra payment? Furthermore, although money will in all probability help to solve some of the widow's problems, it is unlikely to resolve them all. How can the law ensure that these other needs are met? It cannot.

[56] See, for example, *Universe Tankships of Monrovia* v *International Transport Workers' Federation (The Universe Sentinel)* [1983] 1 AC 366.

[57] See, for example, *Royal Bank of Scotland plc* v *Etridge (No 2)* [2001] 4 All ER 449, 457–463, 477–478, 481–483 and 500–503.

[58] See, for example, *Redgrave* v *Hurd* (1881) 20 Ch D 1. There are of course a number of bars to the remedy of rescission and the court has a discretion under section 2 (2) of the Misrepresentation Act 1967 to award damages in lieu of rescission.

[59] The example is based on an illustration used by Charles Fried, *Contract as Promise* (Cambridge, Harvard University Press, 1981), 79.

price for farm land that is far less than the value of land with oil beneath it. The farmer accepts the offer, unaware of the oil under the land. The company does not disclose the discovery of oil prior to entry into the contract. The farmer has now discovered the true position and wishes to set aside the contract. As English law presently stands he would not be able to do so. The company must not tell a lie in order to induce the farmer to enter into the contract, but it is not required to disclose the whole truth. English law does not recognise the existence of a general duty to disclose material facts known to one contracting party but not to the other.[60]

But should the law recognise the existence of a general duty of disclosure? This is a difficult question. On the one hand, it can be argued that the company should be transparent and disclose the information to the farmer prior to entry into the contract. On the other hand, the company may have spent a lot of money acquiring information about the geological make-up of the land. We do not generally require people to give away their assets without charging for them, so why should we require them to give away valuable information for free? While altruism should be encouraged it should not be made compulsory. Transparency is also a good thing, but it should not be mandatory in all cases. In a perfect world we might be entitled to expect, indeed require transparency and full disclosure. But this is not a perfect world and lawmakers and judges cannot assume that it is when they formulate rules of law. It cannot be assumed that the imposition of trustlike obligations is always appropriate in a world in which trust is an increasingly rare commodity.

VI. The Lack of Trust

This leads on to the third point: many contracting parties in the world of commerce enter into contracts because they do not trust each other or because their trust in each other is limited. This is so even in apparently trusting relationships such as joint ventures. To impose on to a contract that has been bargained at arm's length a trusting or loving requirement would be to fail to reflect the expectations of the parties when they entered into the contract. Take the example of a joint venture agreement made between two multinational companies. The operation of the joint venture has not proved to be smooth and the parties have agreed to renegotiate its terms. A lawyer retained by one of the multinational companies advises the company to seek to insert into the joint venture agreement a clause which states that 'it is hereby agreed that neither party shall owe to the other fiduciary duties as a result of entering into this agreement'. Is there anything to be said in favour of the incorporation of such a clause in a contract? In my view there is. It is even-handed in its

---

[60] *Keates* v *Cadogan* (1851) 10 CB 591.

application in that it recognises that neither party owes fiduciary duties to the other. One of its purposes is to ensure that both parties comply with the terms of the contract; in other words, the clause is there to ensure that the contract constitutes the sum total of the rights and liabilities of the parties and that resort cannot be had to fiduciary duties for the purpose of jacking up the obligations of one or other party. Of course it could be argued that the parties ought to be able to trust each other. That may be true but it does not reflect reality in many parts of the world of commerce. Contracts can often be the chosen mechanism of parties who do not trust each other. Any doubtless well-meaning attempt to graft trustlike obligations on to deals marked by a lack of trust is more likely to work mischief than good.[61]

VII. Conclusion

Contract law is firmly rooted in the world as it is and it grapples with many of the problems that arise as a result of our imperfect or fallen nature. A law of contract which assumed that we are omniscient, that we do not pursue self-interest and that we repose complete trust and confidence in our fellow human beings would simply not work. It would not reflect reality and would impose on us obligations with which we could not possibly comply. New Testament principles simply cannot be transplanted directly into the law of contract, nor were they meant to be. Jesus did not come into the world to create a new law of contract and we shall certainly not need the law of contract in heaven. Jesus came to free us from the judgement of the law, not to impose a new law on us. At best we may be able to identify Christian principles or values which should inform our law of contract, but even these can only be identified at a relatively high level of abstraction; for example, that promises should be honoured, lies should not be told, advantage should not be taken of the weak or infirm and respect should be accorded to all men and women as people created in the image of God. But we cannot expect the law of contract to transform the nature of society. One of the lessons of the Old Testament is surely that law cannot change human nature.

But this may be a lesson our society needs to learn. One of the puzzling features of modern society is its apparent willingness to look to the law of contract for a solution to some of society's ills. The scope of contract is extending into areas hitherto the domain of public law. A classic example

[61] Of course, where the parties express themselves in cooperative, trustlike terms there is no objection to the recognition of such obligations because they are consistent with the intention of the parties: cf. *Walford v Miles* [1992] 2 AC 128 where the hostility of the House of Lords towards the duty of good faith and fair dealing appeared to extend to the case in which the parties have expressly assumed an obligation to act in good faith.

was the creation of the internal market in the National Health Service. The reach of contract is now extending into our schools. Recently our children came home with 'home-school agreements' that we, as parents, were required to sign. The document stated that

School will
- encourage children to do their best at all times
- encourage children to take care of their surroundings and others around them
- inform parents of the children's progress at regular meetings
- inform parents about what the teachers aim to teach the children each term
- set regular homework.

This section was signed by the teacher. Turning to the obligations on the other side, the document continued

Family will
- make sure child arrives at school on time – starting at 8.55am
- make sure child attends regularly and provide a note of explanation if child is absent
- attend Consultation Evenings to discuss child's progress
- encourage child to complete homework.

This section was then signed by us as parents. The document concluded

Together we will
- tackle any special needs
- encourage children to work towards the School Aims
- support child's learning to help them achieve their best.

The empire of contract law may soon extend into family life.[62] Anthony Giddens in his book *The Third Way*, after pointing out that marriage and parenthood are becoming disentangled in our society, writes, 'Contractual commitment to a child could thus be separated from marriage, and made by each parent as a binding matter of law, with unmarried and married fathers having the same rights and the same obligations. Both sexes would have to recognize that sexual encounters carry the chance of life-time responsibilities, including protection from physical abuse.'[63]

Leaving to one side this decoupling of marriage and parenthood, one immediate problem that springs to mind when reading this passage relates to the enforcement of these contracts. In what might be thought to be something of an understatement, Dr Giddens continues: 'enforcing parenthood contracts wouldn't be without its problems'.[64]

Why is there this sudden interest in contract law and its extension into areas previously considered to be matters of public service or personal or

[62] An example here might be the renewed interest in antenuptial agreements.
[63] *The Third Way* (Cambridge, Polity Press, 1998), 95.
[64] *Ibid.* at 96.

family matters? This is obviously a difficult question. In relation to the public sector, the answer is in part economic. The government wished to open up the public sector to competitive forces. The aim was presumably to obtain the greater choice, quality and efficiency contracts are alleged to bring. But economics cannot explain its extension into schools and its possible extension into family life. Is there any explanation for this development? The answer is to be found largely in the breakdown of trust between members of society and the modern preoccupation with the assertion of rights. Where relationships are governed by love and trust, there is little or no need for a contract to regulate the relationship between the parties. This argument might appear to be undermined by the fact that the relationship between husband and wife is contractual in nature, but the modern doctrines that make up the law of contract have little application to marriage and it would be surprising if many married couples made use of the law of contract when working out their relationship. The presumption that there is no intention to create legal relations in a domestic context[65] has in the past helped to keep contract in its place 'in the commercial sphere and out of domestic cases, except where the judges think it has a useful role to play'.[66] But as our trust in one another diminishes so we need to find something else to shore up or support the relationship. That 'something else' is increasingly assuming the form of a contract. Contractual thinking also has an emphasis on the assertion of rights ('I am entitled to a given level of service') and an enforcement of responsibilities ('parents shall ensure that their children complete their homework'). As our concern that other people will not discharge their responsibilities to us increases at the same time as our willingness to assert our rights expands, so the law of contract can appear an increasingly attractive institution to regulate relationships between parties in society. But this vision of the law of contract seems to be a long way from Christian principles.

One odd feature of some of these new 'contracts' is that they are not contracts in the eyes of the law. This was true of the internal market in the health service where the aim was apparently to impose the discipline of contracts but not the costs associated with the law of contract.[67] The same is true of the new home-school partnership agreements. While the

---

[65] *Balfour* v *Balfour* [1919] 2 KB 571 ('each house is a domain into which the King's writ does not run').

[66] S. Hedley, 'Keeping Contract in Its Place: *Balfour* v *Balfour* and the Enforceability of Informal Agreements' (1985) 5 *Oxford Journal of Legal Studies* 391.

[67] See, for example, P. Allen 'Contracts in the National Health Service Internal Market' (1995) 58 *Modern Law Review* 321; D. Hughes, J. McHale and D. Griffiths 'Contracts in the NHS: Searching for a Model?' in D. Campbell and P. Vincent-Jones (eds.), *Contract and Economic Organisation* (Aldershot, Dartmouth, 1996), 155.

admission arrangements for a county or voluntary school in England and Wales may provide for home-school partnership documents between the school and the parents, section 413B (6) of the Education Act 1996[68] states that a 'partnership document shall not be capable of creating any obligation in respect of whose breach any liability arises in contract or in tort'. The intention behind the introduction of these new documents is apparently to 'reinforce the relationship between parents and schools by ensuring that parents have a clearer understanding of what the school expects them to do to support their child's education, including disciplinary matters'.[69] Time will tell whether or not these developments achieve their stated goals. I, for one, remain sceptical.

Contracts, whether legally enforceable or not, will not repair the breakdown in relationships we are currently witnessing in society. The heart of the Christian gospel is not that relationships will be transformed by the creation of a new law of contract and an awakened sense of our responsibilities as well as our rights; it is that the restoration of our relationship with God our Father must precede the restoration of our relationships with our fellow human beings. And the restoration of our relationship with God is a matter of grace; it is not a matter for the law of contract. The faith placed by policy-makers in the ability of 'contracts' to transform the nature of relationships in society or to halt their decline is sadly misplaced.

---

[68] Inserted by section 13 of the Education Act 1997.
[69] H L Deb Vol. 578, col. 14 per Lord Henley (10 February 1997).

4

Between a Rock and a Hard Place: Law's Dilemma over Trustees' Ethical Investment

Alison Dunn[1]

> If you have not been trustworthy in handling worldly wealth, who will trust you with true riches? And if you have not been trustworthy with someone else's property, who will give you property of your own?
> Luke 16:9–12

> Honesty and sincerity are not the same as prudence and reasonableness.
> Sir Robert Megarry VC, *Cowan v Scargill* [1985]

I. Introduction

Decades ago, questions about the working conditions of children in third world countries or peasant farmers in Africa and Asia, the erosion of the ozone layer or the content of animal foodstuffs were not ubiquitous. Today, such concerns have become pervasive, extending from the corporate board and the political arena into the supermarket. Disquiet over the consequences of governments' and corporations' policies and practices is no longer expressed by a mere handful of environmental scientists, Christian missionaries or front-line aid workers. Rather, from the school child to the pensioner, by religious and secular campaigning groups, through the provincial newspaper to the World Wide Web, concerns with issues that have become termed 'ethical' or 'socially responsible' are now expressed in the mainstream.

Moves within society to call individuals and organisations to account for their lack of an ethical or socially responsible position are legion.[2] The

---

[1] I am particularly grateful to Paul Beaumont and the anonymous referees for their helpful and constructive comments on an earlier draft of this chapter, the Lawyers' Christian Fellowship Academic conference participants for their discussion of the issues raised by this research, Roderick Paisley for his kind assistance with Scots law sources, and Jeremy Hannah for his research assistance in the summer of 1999.

[2] Spanning from the Nolan/Neill Committee on Standards in Public Life (see First–Sixth Reports [London, HMSO, 1995–99]) to corporate social responsibility. Corporate Social Responsibility is discussed in nn. 74–80

modern market place has become a forum in which organisations' best and worst practices are paraded. In turn this has created an awareness of the influence that may be brought to bear upon governments and other organisations to make reparation for their poor performance. One notable weapon in the financial armoury is the purchasing power represented by individuals' or groups' investment choices. By choosing to reactively disinvest from a particular company on the basis of the company's causation of, or response to, matters of an ethical or socially responsible nature, or by choosing to proactively invest in a company in order to exercise shareholder rights, investors have the potential to influence a company's future direction and so achieve change on a particular issue.

For the individual investor, adopting an ethical position when purchasing company stocks and shares has never been easier. The need for a range of venture strategies that represent clear alternatives to traditional portfolio approaches and that take into account non-financial concerns has led the market to create specific funds that allow investors to select investments from an array of ethical choices. Since 1984, when the first ethical investment unit trust was launched in the UK by Friends Provident, these funds have proliferated, cornering a niche in the market.[3] A gradation of investors with different ethical investment needs can now be catered for through 'light', 'medium' and 'dark green' portfolios depending upon the required level of risk and particular strictness of concern.[4] Figures released from a UK Ethical Investment Research Service (EIRIS), suggest that £2.2 billion was invested ethically in the UK in 1998, a figure that represents an increase of nearly 50 per cent on the previous year.[5] Similarly, figures for the US market indicate a rise to a total

---

[2] (*continued*) below. For a discussion of the different definitions see S. Copp, 'A Christian Vision for Corporate Governance', in P. Beaumont (ed.), *Christian Perspectives on Law Reform* (Paternoster, 1998), 105 at 106–108.

[3] Triodos Bank, for example, operates a Wind Fund that allows investors to support wind farms, and the CF Banner Real Life Investment Trust seeks out companies that publicly profess their commitment to pro-life values, avoiding companies deriving profits from abortion, human embryo research or genetic engineering. See 'New ways to back your beliefs', *Guardian*, 3 October 1998, 6.

[4] See Holden Meehan, *The Millennium Guide to Ethical and Environmental Investment* (London, Holden Meehan, 1998), 16. Investment policies have been variously described as 'positive' or 'negative', 'avoidance', 'alternative' and 'activist', 'reactive', 'proactive' and 'interventionist': see A. Miller, *Socially Responsible Investment: How to Invest With Your Conscience* (New York, New York Institute of Finance, 1991); and R. Sparkes, 'Through a Glass Darkly: Some Thoughts on the Ethics of Investment' (1998) 25(3) *Epworth Review* 13.

5 EIRIS Press Release 27 June 1998. EIRIS was set up in the 1980s with assistance from churches and Christian associations and tracks the prevalence and return of ethical investments within the financial sphere.

of $1,200 billion for the same period.⁶ It is therefore unsurprising that ethical or socially responsible investment is quickly becoming an important facet of the financial markets.

Defining what will be an ethical investment, however, is far from easy, not least because the ambit of the terms 'ethics' and 'ethical' are notoriously difficult to determine. A broad judicial description, adopted for the purposes of this chapter, has allied an ethical investment policy with an approach 'which is not guided solely by financial criteria but which takes into account non-financial considerations deduced from Christian morality'.⁷ Thus investors may choose to invest not solely for the income to be received from share performance, but for the wider benefit of investing in a company which supports personally held principles, thereby enabling the investor both to receive a financial return and to take a moral stand.

Archetypal examples of broad non-financial considerations with a moral flavour that can influence investment choice include a company's exploitation of finite resources including environmental degradation and deforestation; exploitation of the labour force; the promotion of the tobacco industry, gambling or alcohol; involvement in vivisection; the publishing or promotion of pornography; and the funding or provision of arms, or the support of oppressive regimes. More specific to a company's internal procedures, ethical investment can also embrace direct concerns with company policies regarding equal opportunities, including the representation of women on boards of directors or in senior management; directors' remuneration; company donations to political parties or political organisations; company policies on employee age or size; and company involvement within the community.

As noted above, the prevalence of ethical concerns has had a marked impact upon investment opportunities. Correlatively, these opportunities raise questions about investment responsibilities. Although an ethical investment policy is one that can take into account Christian principles, for the Christian, investment has often represented a dilemma and a challenge.⁸ Can money be utilised in a way that allows investment to prevail as a credible expression of faith, or does the first commandment contradict financial trading? Even among Christians opinions diverge on this issue. A study of the investment strategies of Anglican religious communities undertaken in the late 1980s,⁹ for example, revealed views

---

⁶ A. Ashworth, 'How to make your money grow greener', *Times*, 2 June 1999, 15.

⁷ Per Nicholls VC, *Harries v Church Commissioners for England* [1992] 1 WLR 1241 at 1244.

⁸ See B. Seddon, 'Salt and Light – The Challenge of Ethics and Investment' (1997) 24(4) *Epworth Review* 21.

⁹ C. Cowton, 'Where Their Treasure Is: Anglican Religious Communities and Ethical Investment' (1990) *Crucible* April–June 51. The survey concerned

ranging from the absolute that to invest was selfish and that greed should be isolated,[10] to the view that if one was to invest, judgements should not be made of the actions of others, including companies.[11] A more prevalent view, evident from the parable of the ten talents, is one of stewardship:[12] that money should not be buried out of sight but used constructively for its return, financial or otherwise. John Wesley's sermon on 'The Right Use of Money' seems to strike a balance in this uneasy area, and has latterly been used as a rationale for ethical investment.[13] Wesley extolled three basic monetary rules: 'gain all you can ... but not at the expense of life nor at the expense of our health'; 'save all you can'; but crucially, the Christian must also 'give all one can' since 'all of this (gaining and saving) is nothing if a man go not forward, if he does not point all at a farther end'.[14]

While recognising the dilemmas that face the individual Christian investor and the Christian trustee, church groups have in fact been at the forefront of raising the profile of ethical investment and of fostering cogent investment policies. There is, for example, an Ecumenical Committee for Corporate Responsibility, and in 1988 a Christian Ethical Investment Group was set up to promote the ethical investment policy of the Church of England, a body that has also convened a Church Investors Group.

Whatever stance is taken, individual Christians who choose to invest on the basis of non-financial criteria will be supported in their choice by

[9] (*continued*) forty-two religious communities, of which 69 per cent responded to the survey, and 31 per cent actually completed the questionnaire. The primary ranked avoidance investments were gambling, pornography and South African investments, followed by employment issues, environmental issues and tobacco, with advertising complaints, alcohol, animals and arms in joint seventh position. Reference to Cowton's study was first found in R. Sparkes, *The Ethical Investor* (London, HarperCollins, 1995), 7.

[10] Since 'It is easier for a camel to go through the eye of a needle than for a rich man to enter the kingdom of God' (Mark 10:25; Matt. 19:24).

[11] 'Do not judge, or you too will be judged' (Matt. 7:1).

[12] Matt. 25:14–30. See also the chapter by Thomas Watkin in this volume.

[13] Wesley's sermon was based on Luke 16, and is reprinted in *Forty-four Sermons* (Peterborough, Epworth Press, 1974), and cited in Sparkes, 'Through a Glass Darkly', 13. The Government's Pensions Minister, Stephen Timms, used Wesley's sermon as the basis of a lecture to introduce new pensions regulations on ethical investment, discussed below. For a good discussion of Christian attitudes towards money see Sparkes, 'Through a Glass Darkly'; and for a good discussion of Christian involvement in a broad range of ethical/corporate issues see S. Copp, 'A Christian Vision for Corporate Governance', in Beaumont, *Christian Perspectives on Law Reform*, 105.

[14] See also A. De Salins and F.V. De Galhau, *The Modern Development of Financial Activities in the Light of the Ethical Demands of Christianity* (Vatican City, Libreria Editrice Vaticana, 1994).

the developments in the market place. But what of those holding to Christian principles who are required to invest not on their own behalf but for the benefit of third parties? Here the answers are not so straightforward. Should those who control funds on behalf of others, particularly trustees of church, charitable and pension funds, invest in accordance with the principles held by the organisation represented, in accordance with their own moral predilections, or simply in accordance with the financial interests of the fund's beneficiaries? Given the proportion of capital held by trustees on behalf of others, the answer to this question is significant. It is the aim of this chapter to consider the limits of the law with regard to trustees' selection of ethical investment, first by examining the current position on trustees' powers of investment and the ways in which trustees manoeuvre within the law, and secondly, by questioning whether legislation would provide a feasible way forward.

II. Trustee Powers of Investment in English Law

At first glance, English law seems to support the following of Christian principles in the carrying out of trustee duties. The creator of a trust, for example, is free to direct that moral factors be taken into account when investment of the trust fund is undertaken. Case law has consistently emphasised that the trustees' paramount concern when exercising their investment powers lies with the interests of the beneficiaries as dictated by the trust deed and the purpose of the trust. Lord Blackburn explained in *Speight* v *Gaunt*[15] that 'a trustee must not choose investments other than those which the terms of his trust permit'. Thus, where a trust deed authorises trustees to undertake ethical investments, or where the original trust property vested in the trustees contains a share portfolio comprised of or including ethical investments, trustees will be expressly permitted to pursue or consider an ethical policy.[16]

---

[15] (1883) 9 App Cas 1 at 19.
[16] This authorisation is subject to general rules of monitoring and to a duty of care, discussed below. Consider in this respect *Re Harari's Settlement Trusts* [1949] 1 All ER 430, applying *Re Smith* [1896] 1 Ch 71 and *Re McEacharn's Settlement Trusts* [1939] Ch 858, in which Jenkins J construed a clause which allowed trustees to invest 'in or upon such investments as to them may seem fit' as unrestricted, allowing the trustees power to invest in anything they thought to be desirable, irrespective of whether the investments would be authorised by statute. One ground for Jenkins J's decision was that the investments originally held by the fund, that is, left by the testator, were not the type of investments that would have fallen within the authorised range. So a wider investment power can be given either expressly, or by implication in the trust deed.

First glances, however, have a tendency to be misleading, and such is the case in this context. Where a trust deed is silent on the issue, the ability of trustees to employ ethical criteria is far more constricted. Until recently, in the absence of provisions within the trust deed the Trustee Investments Act 1961 provided a statutory scheme for the investment of trust funds. This Act's provisions afforded a rather strict approach to the form of investment that trustees may undertake, and which were categorised into several ranges, each attended by different levels of risk. When investing under this Act, trustees were required under section 6 to seek advice on the suitability of the investments they undertook, and to have regard to diversification of the investment portfolio. Even with the relaxation of the strict investment ranges by the Trustee Act 2000,[17] which repeals the relevant provisions of the Trustee Investments Act 1961 and which, under section 3, now permits trustees to invest in anything they see fit,[18] trustees remain hidebound to financial criteria when investing trust funds.

Crucially, trustees must demonstrate that the trust funds have been managed with due care and skill.[19] The common law standard of care, laid down by the Court of Appeal in *In Re Whiteley*[20] and endorsed upon appeal by the House of Lords,[21] is that of the ordinary prudent man professing the skills of the trustee.[22] Although the common law standard has now been put on a statutory footing under section 1 of the Trustee Act 2000 requiring trustees to 'exercise such care and skill as is reasonable in the circumstances', it does not differ in substance from the common law duty.

Lindley LJ, explaining the common law duty of care in the Court of Appeal, stated that 'The duty of a trustee is not to take such care only as a prudent man would take if he had only himself to consider; the duty

[17] For discussion of these new provisions see the Act's Explanatory Notes, and Law Commission Consultation Paper No. 146, *Trustees' Powers and Duties*, June 1997, and Law Com No 260 *Trustees' Powers and Duties*, 1999.
[18] Pension trustees already had a general power of investment under sections 33–36 Pensions Act 1995.
[19] This standard of care has been recently codified under the Trustee Act 2000, section 1. See discussion below.
[20] (1886) 33 Ch D 347 at 355.
[21] *Learoyd* v *Whiteley* (1887) 12 App Cas 727, where Lord Watson observed (at 733) that 'it is the duty of a trustee to confine himself to the class of investments which are permitted by the trust, and likewise to avoid all investments of that class which are attended by hazard'. This test is an objective test: *Wight* v *Olswang, The Times*, 18 April 2000.
[22] See also *Bartlett* v *Barclays Bank Trust Co. Ltd* [1980] 1 Ch 515. For a comparative discussion of the prudent man rule see G. Palmer, *Trustee Investment: The Relative Merits of the 'Legal List' and 'Prudent Man' Approaches to Trustee Investment*, (Wellington, NZ, Department of Justice, June 1986).

rather is to take such care as an ordinary prudent man would take if he were minded to make an investment for the benefit of other people for whom he felt morally bound to provide.'

Lindley LJ's use of the term 'morally' in this context, however, does not infer an obligation upon trustees to act ethically on behalf of or for the benefit of the beneficiaries. Nor does it seem to provide them with the opportunity so to act. Rather, it confers little more than a requirement to invest with the knowledge that the trust fund is for the benefit of others, and so to ensure that the suitability of an investment is considered, and the portfolio monitored and reviewed. Moreover, it is in considering the suitability of any given investment that trustee duties and ethical issues become polarised. This less than supportive approach is especially evident from the leading English case of *Cowan* v *Scargill*.[23]

In short, *Cowan* v *Scargill* emphasises that the trustees' paramount duty is to act in the best interests of the beneficiaries and so put aside their own moral concerns. *Cowan* concerned the National Coal Board's pension scheme. The scheme's board of management was made up of ten trustees, five each appointed by the Coal Board (CB) and by the National Union of Mineworkers (NUM). An investment plan for the pension scheme was drawn up by the management board in 1980, and revised by the CB trustees in 1982. As a matter of principle and in line with Union policy, the NUM trustees refused to ratify the 1982 investment plan because it included investments in oil and energy companies that were in direct competition with the coal industry, and investments in companies that operated overseas, particularly South Africa. The CB trustees sought directions from the Court.

In holding that the NUM trustees were in breach of their fiduciary duties in holding up implementation of the 1982 investment plan,[24] two specific points emerge from Sir Robert Megarry VC's judgment. First, when complying with the duty of care and acting in the best interests of

---

[23] [1985] 1 Ch 270 Chancery Division. For discussion of this case and the area of ethical investments see G. MacCormack, 'Sexy but not Sleazy: Trustee Investments and Ethical Considerations' (1998) 19 *Company Lawyer* 39; and Lord Nicholls, 'Trustees and Their Broader Community: Where Duty, Morality and Ethics Converge' (1996) 70 *Australian Law Journal* 205.

[24] And that there was no difference between pension trusts and ordinary trusts [1985] 1 Ch 270 at 290. Megarry VC dismissed *Evans* v *London Co-operative Society Ltd, The Times*, 5 July 1976 (Chancery Division) as supporting authority for the NUM position, since the case turned on the facts of the particular pension fund rules. In *Evans* the London Co-operative Society took a number of loans from the pension fund and paid low rates of interest rather than commercial rates. Evans brought an action claiming that the society were in breach of trust in paying those low rates. Brightman J upheld the claim, but on the basis that a properly negotiated agreement between the parties was absent.

the beneficiaries, the benefit afforded by the investment must not be too remote or insubstantial. A tangible link must exist between the purpose of the investment and the benefit of the beneficiaries. For example, a trust for the education of named children in Newcastle that invested part of its trust fund in the only company providing discount computer resources to the beneficiaries' school would arguably afford a link between the investment and the beneficiaries' interests. However, investment by the same trust in another computer company that supported the education of its child labourers in Asia would not have the same ostensible link. A greater sense of moral well-being, which the latter investment may engender, is insufficient in the absence of a tangible benefit to the beneficiaries.[25]

The second point to be drawn from Megarry VC's judgment is that, in assessing the best interests of the beneficiaries, trustees are to have regard to the purpose of the trust. Thus 'When the purpose of the trust is to provide financial benefits for the beneficiaries, as is usually the case, the best interests of the beneficiaries are normally their best financial interests.'[26]

The emphasis upon the beneficiaries' financial interests inevitably means that when acting in a trustee capacity, trustees' moral viewpoints must be subjugated and that, effectively, they are to operate as little more than a conduit for the beneficiaries.[27] Trustees are required to be prudent and reasonable,[28] to consider the relative safety of the capital, the potential yield from the investment and the need for diversification in the investment portfolio.[29] This accords with the trustees' fiduciary duty not

---

[25] On the facts of *Cowan*, prohibiting investment in energy companies and overseas companies did not afford the beneficiaries of the pension fund any direct benefit since, in the view of Megarry VC, 'The connection is far too remote and insubstantial' [1985] 1 Ch 270 at 292–293.

[26] [1985] 1 Ch 270 at 286–287.

[27] Ibid. at 287–288. In Megarry VC's view (at 293) some people are unsuitable to be trustees because they are more concerned with changing the law or policy than acting in the best financial interests of the beneficiaries.

[28] Ibid. at 289.

[29] Re Wragg [1919] 2 Ch 58, Khoo Tek Keong v Ch'ng Joo Tuan Neoh [1934] AC 529. See now Part II, Trustee Act 2000. A comparison with cases such as *Trustees of the British Museum* v *Att-Gen* [1984] 1 All ER 337 shows that this point concurs with general trends in trustee investment law. The court in *British Museum* permitted the variation of a trust fund and an extension of trustees' powers of investment in order that the trust make more financially rewarding investments. Megarry VC (at 342) supported the case for extending trustee powers with four points: the proven responsibility of the trustees; the changed conditions of investment, which require greater choice; the advantage of freedom to invest; and the large size of the trust fund, which called for greater flexibility.

to put themselves in a position where their interests and the interests of the beneficiary conflict.[30] As Templeman J earlier stated in *In Re Wyvern Developments Ltd*,[31] the trustee 'is in a fiduciary capacity and cannot make moral gestures, nor can the court authorise him to do so'.

Megarry VC was willing to accept that in certain, albeit limited, circumstances exceptions could be made to the view that the paramount concern of the trustees lay with the best financial interests of the beneficiaries.[32] These exceptions, however, offer scant additional scope to a trustee seeking to use moral criteria when undertaking investment. According to Megarry VC, non-financial criteria can be taken into account where all the beneficiaries agree,[33] or where the protection of capital and income generation are commensurate between an ethical and a regular investment. In reality, there is little latitude here for the trustee, not least because arriving at a consensus between the beneficiaries of large modern-day trusts is far from feasible, particularly when the trust relates to financial benefits, as with pension funds. Further, while there is evidence to suggest that the position is changing,[34] ethical investments have historically provided the investor with a lower and so incommensurable return as compared with regular investments.

Arguably there appears to be more room to manoeuvre for trustees of charitable trusts, though only because the trust's purpose may not have the same fiscal focus. Sir Donald Nicholls VC accepted in *Harries v Church Commissioners for England*[35] that the paramount concern of charity

---

[30] *Bray v Ford* [1896] AC 44. The other duty is for the fiduciary not to make an unauthorised profit. Megarry VC stated in *Cowan*, 'Powers must be exercised fairly and honestly for the purposes for which they are given and not so as to accomplish any ulterior purposes, whether for the benefit of the trustees or otherwise.' [1985] 1 Ch 270 at 288 citing *Duke of Portland v Topham* (1864) 11 HLCas 32. See comments of Lord Westbury LC in the latter case at 54.

[31] [1974] 1 WLR 1097 at 1106. See also *Buttle v Saunders* [1950] 2 All ER 193 Chancery Division, which involved trustees 'gazumping'. Though note that whereas *Buttle* is often cited as a case requiring trustees to follow a strict approach to getting the best financial return, Wynn-Parry J in fact emphasised (at 195) the point that trustees had a discretion to look at the facts of each case and so to take a balanced approach.

[32] [1985] 1 Ch 270 at 288.

[33] Megarry VC gave the example, *ibid.*, of adult beneficiaries with strict views of moral concerns who 'might well consider that is was far better to receive less than to receive more money from what they consider to be evil and tainted sources'.

[34] See, for example, data from NPI Asset Management's Social Index (www.npi.co.uk); Standard & Poor's Micropal (www.micropal.com); *Social Investment Forum News Release*, Quarter 2, 1998 Fund Performance; *Social Investment Forum News Release*, 25 January 2000, Fund Performance update.

[35] [1992] 1 WLR 1241 Chancery Division.

trustees when exercising their investment duties was to act in the best interests of the beneficiaries using established investment criteria,[36] but that non-financial criteria could be taken into account, where to do otherwise would conflict with the charity's aims, or alienate donors to, or the recipients of, the charity's aid. Notably, Nicholls VC was of the view that this position,[37]

> whilst sound as a matter of legal analysis, is unlikely to arise in practice. It is not easy to think of an instance where in practice the exclusion for this reason of one or more companies or sectors from the whole range of investments open to trustees would be likely to leave them without an adequately wide range of investments from which to choose a properly diversified portfolio.

In *Harries* the investment policy of the Church of England Commissioners had been contested by the Bishop of Oxford who claimed that the Church Commissioners' investment policy attached too great a weight to financial considerations. A declaration was sought that the trustees were obliged to act in a manner compatible with the purpose for which the assets were held, that is, the object of promoting the Christian faith. This declaration was refused by Nicholls VC as being vague and ambiguous.[38] However, he noted in passing that the Church Commissioners were able to pursue an ethical policy because their share portfolio held sufficient quantity of other investments to enable ethical investment to be made without overall financial detriment to the trust fund.[39]

If charity trustees wish to take advantage of the leeway offered in *Harries*, they would also need to ensure that their investment policies did not conflict with their other duties under general charity law.[40] To take one example, if trustees of a charity sought to disinvest from a company that supported or took part in an oppressive governmental regime, or if the charity retained its investment and sought to bring pressure to bear upon the company to change its working practices, the trustees' actions may cross the boundary from permissible ancillary political acts to the prohibited category of substantial political acts.[41] More broadly, charity trustees should remain wary of donors seeking to manipulate

---

[36] *Ibid.* at 1246.
[37] *Ibid.* at 1247.
[38] *Ibid.* at 1252.
[39] R. Nobles has argued that the reasoning in *Harries* produces illogical results. If charities are restricted in investment, why are they not similarly restricted in giving away their funds? See 'Charities and Ethical Investment' (1992) *Conveyancer and Property Lawyer* 115 at 116.
[40] The Charity Commission has published guidance to charities on investment issues: Charity Commission, *Investment of Charitable Funds*, Leaflet CC14 (London, TSO, 1995).
[41] See *Bowman* v *Secular Society Ltd* [1917] AC 406; *National Anti-Vivisection Society* v *IRC* [1948] AC 31; *McGovern* v *Att-Gen* [1982] Ch 321.

the process, by encouraging investment in or disinvestment from certain companies.[42]

Given the context within which the English law of trustee duties operates, the stringency of these rules may appear surprising. English trustees fall within the sphere of Equity. Equity as a body of law is traditionally associated with the remedying of unconscionable conduct, and protection of the vulnerable by providing justice, fairness and even-handedness.[43] Its maxims teach, *inter alia*, that Equity does not suffer a wrong to be without a remedy and looks to substance not to form, expounding the connection between conscience and act. The concern with conscience as a drive for equitable intervention into the common law and the development of Equity's doctrines was partly the result of Christian influence,[44] the tenets of Christianity being one defining ingredient at Equity's inception. Both accentuate qualities of honesty, integrity and guardianship.[45] A residue of the original ecclesiastical influence is still felt in Equity's jurisdictions today, but Equity's allegiance with justice and conscience tends to be based more upon a secular concept of legal obligation than upon more broadly based Christian concerns.

Equity's overall emphasis upon conscience may lead one to assume that trustees would be supported in taking a broad view when undertaking their investment duties. Just as Jesus exhorted the crowds in his sermon on the mount, it would seem indigenous to Equity to exhort trustees to consider the poor, the hungry, lowly, the meek, the victims of injustice, prejudice and persecution.[46]

---

[42] P. Luxton, 'Ethical Investment in Hard Times' (1992) 55 *Modern Law Review* 587 at 590. See also P. Gosling, 'Charities as Social Investors', *NCVO News*, February 1998, 18, who argues that charities are also under pressure not just to invest ethically, but to reduce their reserves and use the money constructively through social investment. See also I. Wall, 'Does your charity take dirty money?' *Big Issue*, 24 January 2000, 19.

[43] For a discussion of the influences that have shaped Equity see A. Dunn, 'Equity is Dead. Long Live Equity!' (1999) 62 *Modern Law Review* 140.

[44] It has been argued by one commentator that the relationship between a priest and God was the first example of a fiduciary relationship, fiduciary duties now being the key to Equity's control of trustees: see S. Herman, 'Utilitas Ecclesiae: The Canonical Conception of the Trust' (1996) 70 *Tulane Law Review* 2239 at 2247. Further, I have noted elsewhere W. Barbour's argument from 'The History of Contract in Early English Equity', in P. Vinogradoff (ed.), *Oxford Studies in Social and Legal History* (Oxford, Clarendon Press, 1914), 150–168, that the equitable remedy of specific performance emerged as a result of the ecclesiastical training of the Lord Chancellors who developed the remedy along the lines of the Christian concept of *fidei laesio*, or breach of faith: see Dunn, 'Equity is Dead', at 147.

[45] Consider, for example, *Bristol & West Building Society* v *Mothew* [1998] Ch 1 at 18.

[46] Matt. 5:3–12; Luke 6:20–23.

As *Cowan* and *Harries* reveal, however, this has proved not to be the case. Rather than a global concern with injustice, Equity's preoccupation with conscience has translated into a direct concern with upholding individual obligations and with refusing to legitimise conduct considered to be reprehensible. When the Lord Chancellor Lord Ellesmere explained in the early part of the seventeenth century that 'the office of the Chancellor is to correct men's consciences for frauds, breach of trusts, wrongs and oppressions, of what nature soever they be',[47] he was restricting concern to the conscience of the individual trustee towards identifiable beneficiaries, rather than towards the correction of wrongs and oppressions at large. Thus rhetoric aside, Equity's concern with justice, not least in the context of trustee investment duties, has been parochially rather than panoramically interpreted.

III. Trustee Powers of Investment in Scots Law

Scots law, while not recognising a body of law called Equity, nevertheless operates the area of trusts and trust investments in a manner similar to that in England. The trust deed is paramount when it comes to the scope for trust investments,[48] and thereafter recourse is made to the Trustee Investment Act 1961.[49] The prudent man rule, which lays down the standard of care, was accepted in *Henderson* v *Henderson's Trustees*.[50] As with English trustees, Scottish trustees will be liable for breach of trust if they fail to invest in accordance with the Act or their standard of care. They will not be absolved liability simply by relying on the practices of other professionals.[51]

The leading Scottish case on ethical investments is *Martin* v *City of Edinburgh District Council*,[52] a case concerned with an action against Edinburgh District Council for breach of fiduciary duty. The council had withdrawn its investments in South African companies as a protest against apartheid. The Court held that a breach of trust had occurred because the Council had failed to take into account the best interests of the

---

[47] *Earl of Oxford's Case* (1615) 1 Ch R 1 at 6.
[48] *Brownlie* v *Brownlie's Trustees* (1879) 6 R. 1233; cf. *Moss's Trustees* v *King*, 1952 SC 523.
[49] Wide powers of investment are not available where a Judicial Factor is appointed by the Court to take care of a fund – *Carmichaels' Judicial Factor*, 1971 SLT 337. A settlor may give wide powers of investment, but where appointed by the court it is the court that gives the powers of investment since it is the court that has to check on the administration.
[50] (1900) 2 F. 1295.
[51] See W. Wilson and A. Duncan, *Trusts, Trustees and Executors* (Edinburgh, W. Green, 2nd ed., 1995), at 420, citing *Alexander* v *Johnstone* (1899) 1 F. 639.
[52] 1988 SLT 329 Outer House.

beneficiaries, or taken professional advice on what would be in the beneficiaries' best interests. In Lord Murray's view,[53] 'under the law of Scotland a trustee's failure to apply his mind properly to a necessary decision is as much a breach of trust as failure to perform a positive duty'.[54]

This was sufficient to decide the point, but Lord Murray went on to consider the English case of *Cowan* v *Scargill*.[55] He pointed out, strictly *obiter*, that seeking the best financial return required trustees to be more involved than simply approving without question the financial advice that they received.[56] Moreover, trustees have a duty not to fetter their discretion with a decision *ab ante* and a duty not to fetter discretion for reasons beyond the trust's purpose. Lord Murray thought that while it may not always be possible for a trustee to be divorced from political beliefs or conscience,[57]

> What he must do ... is to recognise that he has those preferences, commitments or principles but, nonetheless, do his best to exercise fair and impartial judgments on the merits of the issue before him. If he realises that he cannot do that, then he should abstain from participating in deciding the issue ... or, in the extreme case, resign as a trustee.

IV. Trustee Powers of Investment in United States Law

The position in American law is as restrictive as that in England and Scotland.[58] There is no statute similar to that of the Trustee Investments Act 1961 or the Trustee Act 2000 to regulate authorised investments, but the law operates around a state-based 'prudent investor rule', which

---

[53] *Ibid.* at 334.

[54] The trustees must actively consider investment, that is, they have a duty to consider exercising their investment powers: *Melville* v *Nobles Trustees* (1896) 24 R. 243 Second Division (trustees had left the trust fund in a deposit bank account for twenty years, yielding a low rate of return), and that the investment must yield a return (*Moss's Trustees v King*, 1952 SC 523. In the English context, see also *Re Wragg* [1919] 2 Ch 58).

[55] An example of a case where fund maximisation was not an issue is *Fraser* v *Paterson (No. 2)*, 1988 SLT 124 Outer House, which concerned the estate of an incapax. One English case on Local Authority disinvestment was *The Queen* v *London Borough of Lewisham, ex parte Shell* (1990) Pensions Law Reports 217 in which disinvestment by the local authority was held to be ultra vires, on the basis that the decision on disinvestment had been taken in the absence of good faith.

[56] 1988 SLT 329 at 334.

[57] *Ibid.* at 334.

[58] Though not bound by American law, Megarry VC in *Cowan* in fact drew upon the American position to support his own decision: see [1985] 1 Ch 270 at 292.

lays down a minimum standard of care for trustees to uphold. The prudent investor rule stems from *Harvard College* v *Amory*[59] and has been adopted in the majority of states. The formulation of Judge Putnam in *Harvard College*[60] is that a trustee should 'conduct himself faithfully and exercise sound discretion. He is to observe how men of prudence, discretion and intelligence manage their own affairs, not in regard to speculation, but in regard to the permanent disposition of their funds, considering the probable income, as well as the probable safety of the capital to be invested.'

The prudent investor rule appears to encompass three notions, those of care, caution and judgement.[61] It will not be breached where the cost of a socially responsible investment is de minimis,[62] or where so to invest would protect the capital of the fund as in the case of *Withers* v *Teachers' Retirement System of the City of New York*.[63] *Withers* concerned the decision of trustees to purchase highly speculative New York City Bonds, justified on the basis that since the City was a major contributor to the Teachers' Retirement System pension fund, the purchase of the bonds guaranteed the payment of pension benefits. The District Court of New York held that the purchase by five pension funds of the unmarketable New York Bonds for the purpose of staving off the bankruptcy of New York City council, was acceptable on the basis that the investment had been undertaken by the trustees in the best interests of the beneficiaries, rather than for wider concerns of public welfare or protection of jobs.[64] The use of ethical criteria here was thus justified on financial grounds.

---

[59] 26 Mass (9 Pick) 446 (1830). See also *King* v *Talbot* 40 NY 76 at 85–86 (1869).

[60] *Ibid.* at 461.

[61] See the commentary of G. Bogert, D. Oaks, H. Hansen and C. Hill, *Cases and Text on the Law of Trusts* (New York, The Foundation Press, 6th ed., 1991), 329. In the case of American pension funds, the section 404 (a) (1) of the Employee Retirement Income Security Act 1974 (ERISA) lays down a prudent investor rule and dictates that actions should be taken by fund trustees solely in the interests of the beneficiaries. This would preclude socially responsible investment on any other criteria than financial. For a consideration of ERISA see L. Irish and A. Kent, 'The Social Investing Quandary: May Investment Fiduciaries Consider Non-financial Factors in Making Pension Investments' (1994) 8 *Trust Law International* 10.

[62] *Board of Trustees of Employees Retirement System* v *Mayor and City Council of Baltimore* 317 Md 72, 562 A. 2d 720 (1989), Maryland Court of Appeal.

[63] 447 F Supp 1248 (1978).

[64] *Ibid.* at 1256, 1259. Consider also *Blakenship* v *Boyle* 329 F Supp 1089 (1971) US District Court of Columbia, which concerned a welfare fund for present and future coal miners. A number of actions were brought against the trustees, but one for breach of trust related to the investment by the trustees in a number of public utilities, the shares of which had decreased in value.

Similar to the English position under *Cowan* and *Harries*, the American Restatement on Trusts permits social or political views to influence investment choice where authorised by the trust document or the trust's beneficiaries, or where, in a charitable trust, the investment advances the charitable purpose 'financially or operationally'.[65]

V. Options

Trustee investment duties in English, Scots and United States law ostensibly leave the trustee who is committed to moral concerns with little solace. Lord Murray's approach, that trustees who are unable to put aside their moral concerns should either abstain from participation or resign, is hardly appealing, particularly in the case of trustees of church or charitable funds.[66] Given the state of the law, how do trustees who wish to follow Christian principles reconcile investment with duty, and financial purpose with conscience?

The answer to this question reveals a paradox: that despite the rather strict approach taken by the law, a comparatively high level of ethical investment is nonetheless pursued. For example, in 1996 EIRIS undertook a survey of ninety-eight well-known charities including the Top Fifty charities by legacy and voluntary income.[67] Of the sixty-two charities that responded, 37 per cent had a formal ethical investment policy, that is, one agreed by trustees; 18 per cent had an informal ethical investment policy, which meant that decisions may be affected by ethical considerations, but no formal policy was agreed by trustees; and 8 per cent indicated that the question of adopting a formal ethical investment policy was to be considered by trustees within the next 12 months. In addition, 15 per cent of the respondents had a policy to screen donors on ethical grounds.

---

[64] (*continued*) The investments had been made with the purpose of forcing more companies to burn coal and so to protect the jobs within the coal industry. The court found against the trustees on the basis of self-dealing and therefore breaching the loyalty part of the prudent investor rule.

[65] *Restatement of the Law on Trusts (Third)* (St Paul, Minn., American Law Institute, 1992).

[66] *Martin v Edinburgh District Council* 1988 SLT 329 at 334. This point is important when one considers the impression that churches give to society when their portfolios are revealed. The Church of England, for example, was the subject of a recent protest by the lobby group Mutual Assistance for Investors & Account Holders (MAFIA) on account of the shares held by the Commissioners in the banking sector at a time when the sector is under attack for its procedures, see 'Cross purposes', *Guardian*, 21 April 2000, 29.

[67] *Well-Known Charities and Ethical Investment: A Summary of Survey Results*, EIRIS Press Release, 11 July 1997.

Furthermore, the majority of Christian denomination churches in the UK[68] either have a formal policy that includes ethical criteria for their investments, or have established rules of thumb, both of which are monitored by trustees and kept under regular review.[69] Not all these policies are centrally determined or decreed. Rather, some denomination churches, such as the United Reformed Church, have advisory guidelines on ethical investment that are provided to regional church groups. The most common practice appears to be for church trustees to screen out certain categories of companies when undertaking investment (common exclusions include companies deriving profit from tobacco, alcohol, gambling or pornography), although some trustees also employ positive criteria in investment selection.[70] Trustees of church funds have also been expeditious in disinvesting from companies when necessary.[71] Thus the answer to the question of how trustees can uphold their views lies in the

[68] All Christian denomination churches were contacted in the summer of 1999 by the author and information was requested on ethical investments policies, including whether guidelines were issued to individual diocese, the types of ethical investments undertaken, or non-ethical investments avoided, and the proportion of funds devoted to ethical investments. All but one denomination church responded. The author is grateful to all the respondents, and in particular to David Holmes, Religious Society of Friends in Britain; Rev. Peter Brain, Secretary for Church and Society, United Reformed Church; Andrew Atkinson, Trust Officer of The United Reformed Church (Northern Province) Trust Ltd; Mr John Henderson, Secretary to The Church of Scotland Investors Trust; Mr W.T. Seddon, Investment Manager, Central Finance Board of the Methodist Church; Col. Gordon Becker, Secretary for Business Administration, The Salvation Army; Antony Hardy, Investment Manager and Secretary to the Ethical Investment Working Group, The Church Commissioners, Church of England.

[69] The Central Finance Board of the Methodist Church, for example, has a mission statement declaring its aims 'to provide a high quality investment service seeking above average financial returns for investors; to follow a discipline in which the ethical dimension is an integral part of all investment decisions; to construct investment portfolios which are consistent with the moral stance and teachings of the Christian faith; to encourage strategic thinking on the ethics of investment and to be a Christian witness in the investment community'.

[70] The Church Commissioners for the Church of England, for example, have recently moved to both negative and positive criteria. They have also moved from a banned sector approach to assessing companies on an individual basis: *Ethical Investment Working Group, Second Report to the General Synod* (GS Misc 521, 18 May 1998) (London, General Synod of Church of England, 1998).

[71] A number of church groups disinvested from BSkyB in the mid 1990s when the company took over the Playboy Channel, and from Total in 1997 on account of human rights abuses in Burma.

fact that, in no small part, the concern of church groups with fusing faith with finance has led trustees to seek ways in which they can legitimately manoeuvre around the law's grey environs.

VI. Finding God in the FTSE 100

When Nicholls VC in *Harries v Church Commissioners for England* explained that trustees of charitable trusts could exceptionally employ non-financial criteria to select investments, where to do otherwise would alienate those most likely to donate to the charity,[72] he was applying sound financial principles. It is important for trustees to safeguard the capital of the trust fund, and alienating those most likely to contribute to that fund would not be prudent.[73] Moral issues can thus have a direct place in trustee investment portfolios where they can be located within financial parameters. Two methods stand out in particular as ways in which trustees can manipulate their investment focus. These are assessment of a company by its products, processes and affiliations, and the exercise of shareholder rights.

The trustees' paramount concern is with the benefit of the beneficiaries and, as noted above, that benefit is assessed in the light of the purpose of a trust. As the majority of trusts exist to afford fiscal benefits, trustees are required to look to financial indicators when considering the suitability of an investment. In this regard the prudent trustee will seek advice and take a range of factors into account. The position of the company in the market, predicted growth, profit margins and share performance are obvious criteria. But trustees need also to consider whether there are any factors in the company's products, working processes or affiliations which have the potential to affect future share value. Companies, for example, that operate at the law's margins, or in contentious areas, could be the subject of legal penalty or targets for consumer boycott.[74] Thus for financial reasons it may not be prudent to invest in companies that do not follow a practice of what has been latterly termed 'corporate social responsibility', or which for other reasons fall outside the legal or social boundaries set for acceptable practices.

---

[72] [1992] 1 WLR 1241 at 1247. A point certain anti-smoking charities have found to their cost when it was revealed that their investment portfolios contained investments in tobacco: 'Cancer charities invest in Tobacco', *Sunday Times*, 14 May 1995; 'Smoke gets in your portfolio', *Guardian*, 27 March 1996.

[73] The same would apply to contributory pension trusts.

[74] Consider liability for pollution or the recent furore over genetically modified crops and foodstuffs. See, S. Tromans, 'Environmental Responsibility and Shareholder Expectations – 1', *New Law Journal*, 24 October 1997, 1540 at 1541; 'Directors' Responsibilities and Shareholders' Wishes – 2', *New Law Journal*, 9 January 1998, 21.

The significance of this point is not to be underestimated. Awareness of the need for corporate social responsibility has increased dramatically in the last decade,[75] and a growing number of organisations have issued guidelines and codes of practice for ethical business operations.[76] From the trustees' point of view, corporate social responsibility can often resonate with their own moral beliefs. For example, while not strictly defined, one working formulation identifies corporate social responsibility with a concern for 'the continuing commitment by business to behave ethically and contribute to economic development while improving the quality of life of the workforce and their families as well as of the local community and society at large'.[77]

Moreover, this concern with corporate actions within the wider market place may itself force change. Both the World Business Council for Sustainable Development[78] and the Turnbull Working Party on

[75] There are a number of organisations promoting corporate social responsibility, including the Institute of Social and Ethical Accountability; Coalition for Environmentally Responsible Economies (CERES); Global Reporting Initiative; Ecumenical Council for Corporate Social Responsibility. Corporate social responsibility, however, has both proponents and objectors: cf. C. Handy, 'What Is a Company for?' *RSA Journal*, March 1991; and M. Friedman, *Capitalism and Freedom* (Chicago, University of Chicago Press, 1962). Although recent research suggests that companies pursuing ethical practices can boost profits: M.V. Russo and P.A. Fouts, 'A Resource-Based Perspective on Corporate Environmental Performance and Profitability' (1997) 40 *Academy of Management Journal* 534. See also S. Copp, 'A Christian Vision for Corporate Governance', in Beaumont, *Christian Perspectives on Law Reform*, 105.

[76] For example, Amnesty International UK has developed a code on Human Rights Guidelines for Companies; the European Union Parliament has developed a European Corporate Code of Conduct; the International Chamber of Commerce has a Charter for Sustainable Development, and the Department for International Development has an Ethical Trading Initiative. For further details see P. Watts and R. Holme, *Meeting Changing Expectations: Corporate Social Responsibility* (Geneva, WBCSD, 1999), Appendix 1; C. Ferguson, *A Review of UK Company Codes of Conduct* (London, DFID, 1998).

[77] WBCSD Stakeholder Dialogue on Corporate Social Responsibility, The Netherlands, 6–8 September 1998.

[78] Watts and Holme, *Meeting Changing Expectations*. This report identifies (p. 2) as priority areas human rights, employee rights, environmental protection, supplier relations and community involvement. Other points identified by the report (p. 11) as integral to any corporate social responsibility strategy are helping societies develop the capacity to build themselves; taking a long-term view with long-term commitment; building corporate/community partnerships; cooperating on technology; showing transparency in corporate affairs and making responsibility an integral part of the company's ethos, as opposed to a public relations exercise.

Internal Controls of companies, which published consultative guidance on the 1998 Combined Code on Corporate Governance,[79] have warned that companies must be alive to the need to assess the risks they run from not being socially responsible, particularly in terms of reducing profits and the value of shareholders' investments. Thus where a company's products, processes or affiliations impact upon share performance, trustees have legitimate grounds to avoid share purchase or to disinvest.[80]

Further, it is well to note that the investment process does not stop upon share purchase, and share ownership does not rest with financial return. An ethical investment policy can extend beyond concern with the actual shares purchased. Shareholders are the subject of other rights and have clear opportunities to influence the direction of a company. This can occur within or outwith the formal bounds of a company's annual general meeting. The Church of England Church Commissioners, for example, have a long history of entering into both formal and informal negotiations with the companies with which they have a shareholding, in order to press for change to company policy or practice.[81] Thus, even where trustees hold investments that are out of line with their moral principles, they can, providing they do not go beyond their fiduciary duties, use their voting rights or their position as a shareholder to enter into constructive dialogue with the company.[82]

The ability of trustees so to act has particular importance in those cases where funds are delegated to independent fund managers. It has been

---

[79] *Internal Control: Guidance for Directors of Listed Companies Incorporated in the UK*, Consultation Draft, April 1999. See *Guardian*, 24 April 1999, 26. The Combined Code on Corporate Governance was produced by the Hampel Committee on Corporate Governance's *Final Report* (London, Gee, 1998), continuing recommendations from The Committee on the Financial Aspects of Corporate Governance, *Report and Code of Best Practice* (the 'Cadbury Report') (London, Gee, 1992), and the Study Group on Directors' Remuneration's *Report on Directors' Remuneration* (the 'Greenbury Committee') (London, Gee, 1995).

[80] A long way from *Cowan* v *Scargill*, in May 1999, for example, British Coal Pension Fund launched a screening assessment of its portfolio specifically pertaining to the environmental impacts of investments. It justified its action on financial grounds, that is, a pollutant company runs the risk of liability and so will affect long-term profits. See 'Leading pension fund intends to assess its environmental impact' (1999) *Ethical Investor* May/June, 1.

[81] For example, the Church Commissioners' negotiations with Shell, which led to Shell entering into constructive dialogue with local churches in Nigeria is one example. See, B. Seddon, 'Salt and Light – The Challenge of Ethics and Investment' (1997) 24(4) *Epworth Review* 21 at 22–23.

[82] As Barclays Bank found to their cost on deciding to close almost two hundred of its rural branches: 'Middle England forces Barclays to say sorry', *Independent*, 27 April 2000.

pointed out in the US context[83] that fund managers who vote on proxy for trust funds often side with company management. This may not be ethically acceptable or, crucially, in the beneficiaries' best interests. Trustees can and should take a more active role in the exercise of their share voting rights rather than to leave them to their delegate.

Exercise of shareholder rights and assessing companies by their products, processes and affiliations provide trustees with viable options to bring ethical issues into their investment decisions. However, as measures these alternatives are no more than short term and do not obviate the law's primary concentration upon financial return. Examining a company's corporate social responsibility, for example, will not exclude enough companies to leave only ethical options, and voting on an issue in a company's AGM will not guarantee change. In addition trustees may find that creeping along the law's boundaries is not always a comfortable place to be, particularly when investments fail, or when decision-making processes are open for scrutiny.

Where is the limit of the law in this context? From Equity's point of view, in a sector still reeling from the Maxwell pensions debacle, fund security and the protection of trust beneficiaries from risk, deception or manipulation are essential. There would appear to be little room for movement on ethical investments in an area focused so tautly on accountability.[84] Is it feasible for another way forward to be forged?

VII. The Way Forward

If ethical investment represents a conscionable approach to money management and resource allocation, should the law via legislation provide trustees with greater powers of control over their investment decisions and in the monitoring of their portfolios? More radically, given the sea change in society, should trustees be compelled to undertake investment based on ethical criteria?

The potential latitude offered by legislation may be readily accepted by those seeking a more panoramic approach than is provided by Equity's parochial focus. At the very least, allowing trustees the direct opportunity when choosing investments to weigh up interests that have hitherto been perceived as competing is attractive, particularly from a Christian viewpoint. Legislation too, could provide much needed certainty for

---

[83] M. Curzon and M. Pelesh, 'Revitalising Corporate Democracy: control of Invest Managers' Voting on Social Responsibility Proxy Issues' (1980) 93 *Harvard Law Review* 670.

[84] Lord Nicholls also argued, in an extrajudicial context, that because the Equity is concerned with duties and responsibilities, its boundaries should be certain and clear, 'Trustees and Their Broader Community: Where Duty, Morality and Ethics Converge' (1996) 70 *Australian Law Journal* 205 at 207.

beneficiaries and trustees alike in this ambiguous area. But while statutory provisions could offer advantages by way of transparency or succour to the trustee seeking to follow Christian principles, the introduction of legislation in this area could also represent a Pandora's box.

Notwithstanding questions over whether law's role is to facilitate or coerce, the primary problems raised by legislation concern those of terminology, definition, and determining boundaries. It has already been noted that it is notoriously difficult to render precise the terms 'ethics' and 'ethical', and in this context the draftsman's task would be an onerous one.[85] Ethical principles are varied and variable,[86] and while this factor alone may not be enough to decry legislation, it does attest to the obstacle of diversity. It also raises the exigency of establishing and implementing enforcement procedures and penalties.

Further, legislation brings forward the problem of arbitrariness. Should a statutory scheme introduce a quantitative or a qualitative approach? If quantitative, should trustees be permitted to devote a proportion of their funds, say 20 per cent, to ethical investment? Or should only those trust funds over a certain capital or income threshold be authorised to devote their funds to investments based on ethical criteria? Alternatively, if the approach is to allow for a more balanced and qualitative strategy, one is brought back to the issue of defining parameters and of trustees acting by lip-service to a legislative requirement rather than substantive concern with genuine ethical issues. Indeed, it is hard to see how a qualitative strategy would operate as a legislative provision. Is the law to be concerned with only those trust funds with enough purchasing power to enforce change?[87] Again, what would be the enforcement mechanisms or penalty bases?

---

[85] Nicholls VC's view in *Harries* v *Church Commissioners for England* [1992] 1 WLR 1241 at 1252 that a declaration to invest in line with 'Christian principles' would be too ambiguous is illustrative of this point.

[86] Even within the construct of Christian morality, multifarious views exist, particularly on issues such as alcohol consumption or abortion. Another issue has often beleaguered trustees of church funds: whether it is ethical to invest in armament companies. See discussion of Nicholls VC in *Harries ibid.*, at 1247–1248, 1251.

[87] Megarry VC in *Cowan* v *Scargill* [1985] 1 Ch 270 at 295, seemed to suggest that a qualitative ethical strategy would be acceptable where it could effect change, though his emphasis was on the fact that this would be because it would turn a benefit which would otherwise be too remote into something tangible. This approach also had support from Megarry VC in *Trustees of the British Museum* v *Att-Gen* [1984] 1 All ER 337 where he was of the view (at 343) that 'A fund that is very large may well justify a latitude of investment that would be denied to a more modest fund; for the spread of investments possible for a larger fund may justify the greater risks that wider powers will permit to be taken.'

Of these two alternative legislative strategies, quantitative against qualitative, the former would be the least attractive. Not only would it be overly restrictive, harking back to the rigid and much criticised approach of the Trustee Investments Act 1961, but if the law is to accept that ethical investment is a valid option for trustees it should not have to place artificial restrictions on the amount of funds used in its pursuit. Either trustees' ethical investment is recognised as judicious, or it isn't.

Furthermore, with regard to legislative pitfalls, not only is it difficult in terms of clarity and precision to provide for or compel ethical investment, but it is also ultimately difficult to assess the ethical claims of companies or investment funds,[88] not least because one consumer's ethical principle is another company's profit margin. Bandwagon marketing has the potential to escalate as it becomes clear that ethical products and practices are in themselves a commodity.[89] In such circumstances, assessing whether trustees have complied with statutory provisions will be almost impossible.[90]

Clearly, legislation is attended with difficult questions as to the scope, reach and enforceability of statutory provisions. However, one must not lose sight of the fact that the difficulties identified above pertain to statutory form, not to the substance of the question whether the law should permit or prohibit trustees from undertaking ethical investments. Despite the difficulties, one of our tasks as Christians is to push the limit of the law relentlessly, not least because the pertinence of the legal system to involve itself with balancing beneficiaries' and trustees' concerns is not diminished simply because it is hard to draw up a workable solution.

Of course, an alternative approach that would expedite ethical investment for trustees who wish the law to be no more than facilitative, is for legislation simply to set no greater boundary than that trustees may make any investment they see fit. This obviates problems of definition and thresholds, and of ensuring compliance. The new Trustee Act 2000 carries through this approach. However, the Act also puts on a statutory footing the trustees' duty of care, and herein lies the rub. It has to be remembered that trustees hold funds for the benefit of third parties who will be particularly vulnerable to their actions. It is largely insignificant

---

[88] Consider, for example, 'Are Ethical Investors Being Green', *Labour Research*, Vol. 80, July 1991, 13.

[89] See, for example, the report that accountancy firms are being used to help companies develop 'ethical risk strategies': J. Kelly, 'Bottom line on ethical auditing', *Financial Times*, 9 September 1999, 12.

[90] A further point made by the British Columbia Law Institute's Committee on the Modernization of the Trustee Act in their *Report on Trustee Investment Powers* (Vancouver, British Columbia Law Institute, 1999) was that a legislative provision 'would not be likely to send the correct message' to trustees in that it would divert focus from the more immediate financial purposes: 20.

from the beneficiaries' point of view what investments trustees are permitted to undertake. What is significant, however, is that beneficiaries have recourse to a duty of care to safeguard their position. Here is the law's dilemma. Without a duty of care, how are trustees to be monitored? With a duty of care, how are trustees to be monitored without reference to the financial indicators that restrict investment in ethical funds that are non-commensurate with regular investments, as at present? It is already difficult for beneficiaries to question trustee decisions,[91] but at least the financial yardstick provides them with leverage. Even if trustees are judged by their fiduciary duties alone, the duty not to put themselves in a position where their interests and those of the beneficiaries conflict, brings once more to the fore the question of the criteria to be applied in assessing the beneficiaries' interests. The conundrum that seems impregnable is how to provide trustees with latitude in the ethical arena without also compromising the beneficiaries' security.[92]

The above analysis reveals the central problem in testing the limit of the law in this arena. The ethics of trustee investment are complex, and ethical investment *per se* is just one aspect of a broad range of issues facing trustees. It is not just investment return at any price that exercises the faith of a Christian trustee, and it is not just beneficiary protection at any cost that exercises the law's boundaries. Quandaries exist between beneficiary protection and trustee innovation, investment regulation and market freedom, short-term benefits and long-term risk, investment gain and capital protection. The dilemmas are many, and the law is faced with substantive questions concerning the compromise to be made between beneficiary and trustee, profit and principle, and in whose favour that compromise is to be drawn.

Ultimately, law's teeth sit in the jaws of society and trustee investment may be an arena where legislative impotency is countered by social pressure. The shift in contemporary western society from the boom of company profits and 'fat cat' salaries in the 1980s, to public accountability, regional regeneration, citizenship and corporate social responsibility is tangible. It could well be that social and political pressure represents the greatest force in forging the way forward for those seeking greater opportunity to undertake ethical investment.[93] At the beginning of the

---

[91] *Nestle* v *National Westminster Bank plc* [1994] 1 All ER 118 sets up a causation test, and *Wight* v *Olswang, The Times*, 18 April 2000 more recently has emphasised that trustee investment decisions will not constitute a breach of trust where they are considered 'reasonable'.

[92] Legislative provisions have been accepted in Manitoba, but were more recently rejected in British Columbia, see Committee on the Modernization of the Trustee Act, *Report on Trustee Investment Powers* (Vancouver, British Columbia Law Institute, 1999).

[93] See generally, T. Gorringe, *Fair Shares: Ethics and the Global Economy* (London, Thames & Hudson, 1999). Ed Mayo, Executive Director of the

year 2000, for example, the Chancellor of the Exchequer, Gordon Brown, announced the creation of a new Social Investment Task Force, the purpose of which is to examine how social investment can be fostered in the UK.[94] An All Parliamentary Group on Socially Responsible Investment had been set up in January 1998 to promote discussion on ethical investment issues, notably in the legislative process. These bodies are augmented by the work of the UK Social Investment Forum, the European Forum on Social Investment, and the International Association of Investors in Social Economy.

Significantly, trustees of pension funds have joined these actors in this social debate. Following on from consultation to a pensions green paper in 1998,[95] a new regulation under the Pensions Act 1995 came into force on 3 July 2000. This regulation requires pension scheme trustees to disclose in their Statement of Investment Principles the extent to which, if at all, they take ethical and social considerations into account in the selection and management of their investment policies, or in the exercise of their shareholder rights.[96] This regulation does not change trust law. It does not alter the trustees' duty of care, nor their primary focus on the best interests of the beneficiaries as discerned from the purpose of

---

[93] (continued) New Economics Foundation, for example, has identified six key features explaining the growth of social investment: withdrawal of the nation state from direct provision; changes in state policy; growth of an ethical new economy; hyper-competition; information and disclosure; and emerging investment niches. E. Mayo, 'The Future for Social Investment', speech given to the UK Social Investment Forum Conference, July 1999.

[94] Announced at the National Council for Voluntary Organisations Annual Conference, 9 February 2000. For the text of the Chancellor's speech see www.hm-treasury.gov.uk/speech/cx90200.html. This Task Force is to be run in partnership with the UK Social Investment Forum and the New Economics Foundation.

[95] *A New Contract for Welfare: Partnership in Pensions* Cm 4179, December 1998. See in particular paragraphs 68–69.

[96] The Statutory Instrument (SI 1999, No. 1849) amends the Occupational Pension Schemes (Investment) Regulations 1996 with the insertion of regulation 11A: 'The matters prescribed for the purposes of section 35 (3) (f) of the 1995 [Pensions] Act (other matters on which trustees must state their policy in their statement of investment principles) are – (a) the extent (if at all) to which social, environmental or ethical considerations are taken into account in the selection, retention and realisation of investment; and (b) their policy (if any) in relation to the exercise of the rights (including voting rights) attaching to investments.' Trustees are already required under section 35 of the Pensions Act 1995 to prepare, maintain and revise the pension scheme's Statement of Investment Principles (SIP). Section 35 (2) (b) of the Pensions Act states that trustees must have a policy, but are not required to actively invest.

the trust. Rather, the objective of the regulation is to 'stimulate debate on socially responsible investment further and increase transparency in investment planning'.[97]

While it is hard to see the utility of a regulation that aims to make pension trustees disclose their policies on an area they are prohibited to consider directly under trust law, it may at least focus trustee minds on the ethics of the companies they invest in. An Ethical Pensions Learning Network has already been set up, and at least one pension trust has declared its interest in appointing a member of staff to look at ethical issues.[98] In today's social environment where consumer action and environmental concern have become *de rigueur*, compliance by market example, and change forced by social movement may in the end win the day.

VIII. Conclusion

At the beginning of the last decade, *Nestle v National Westminster Bank plc* highlighted how trusts and trustee duties had developed from the Victorian period.[99] Dillon LJ, for example, noted that while 'Trustees should not be reckless with trust money ... what the prudent man should do at any time depends on the economic and financial conditions of that time – not on what judges of the past, however eminent, have held to be the prudent course in the conditions of 50 or 100 years ago.'[100]

In the view of the contemporary judiciary, the most prudent course for trustee investment is for trustees, at best, to divorce themselves from their morals or, at least, to subjugate their principles in favour of profit margins. For anyone committed to their personal beliefs, this edict represents a formidable task not necessarily advantageous for trustees, beneficiaries or for the efficacy of the law. Those committed to the pursuit of an ethical investment policy based on Christian principles or other personally held beliefs, have long witnessed the growth of free trade and questioned the

---

[97] Stephen Timms, Pensions Minister, Department of Social Security Press Release, 1 July 1999.

[98] The University Superannuation Scheme (USS) is the third largest occupational pension in the UK. It has 140,000 members and assets of around £16 billion. Over the past few years it has been lobbied extensively by Ethics for USS, calling for more transparency and openness in investment policies and portfolio. In the USS's Institutions meeting in December 1999 it agreed to pursue a policy of 'more active engagement' (Sir Graeme Davies, Chair) – creating a specific post to liaise with companies and other pension investors and to closely monitor companies and enter into a constructive dialogue. For comment see, G. Hughes, 'When ethics wins the pensions fund debate', *Times Higher Education Supplement*, 17 December 1999, 14.

[99] [1994] 1 All ER 118 at 139 per Leggatt LJ.

[100] *Ibid.* at 126.

role of all actors in the process. Yet in the wider legal arena investment based on anything other than financial criteria is still an embryonic notion. Moves within the market place may well mean that this position alters and that changes to company practices forced by social pressure and wider Christian action make ethical investment a more prudent course in years to come. As a consequence, greater social awareness of ethical practices may also assist settlors and, more importantly, their legal advisors, in making ethical investment an integral component of their trust deeds.

In the meantime trustees remain between a rock and hard place, neither able to pursue a working faith, nor able to ignore the consequences of their actions. But possibly the greatest limit to the law in this arena is that of passivity. Given the obstacles in the way of legislative change, and the legal dilemmas presented by trustee investment, it would be easy to step back and rely on pressure from the social environment to force development in trust law at some indeterminate time in the future. Yet although legislation in this area would be beset by difficulties, this does not invariably mean that there is no place for law reform. Since ethical investment is about careful judgement, not demarcating investments into good or bad,[101] there is, perhaps, greater scope for the judiciary to be more sensitive to the fine balancing act that trusteeship dictates in terms of investment practice. Dillon LJ's exhortation of the need to be mindful of changing portfolio strategies and of the shifting categorisation of prudence should be borne in mind, not as a retrospective rhetorical observation of social change, but as unequivocal advice to the judiciary to take cognisance of alternative investment approaches.

Few would argue with the view that flexibility and judicial discretion have long been seen as one of Equity's hallmarks. Building upon that already existing foundation, a tentative solution in this area would be for the courts to take a more inquiring approach to assessing the trustees' duty of care. At present the inquiry made is one into whether trustees have been prudent in their investment strategies. As noted above, this notion of prudence is founded upon financial criteria, and upon whether the trustees have acted in the 'usual course of business'.[102] It is understandable that the courts have taken this approach and, as explained earlier, it at least provides beneficiaries with leverage in challenging trustee actions. Yet the use of financial considerations as the *sole* criteria has had the tendency to polarise ethical investment into stark questions that divide profit from principle. At this juncture the fluidity of a Christian approach to trustee investment is lost. The Christian approach is not to pursue justice in one arena (investment) at the expense of the

---

[101] Consider D. Anderson, *What Has 'Ethical Investment' to Do with Ethics?* (London, Social Affairs Unit St Edmundsbury Press Ltd, 1996), 4.

[102] See discussion of Lord Watson in *Learoyd* v *Whiteley* (1887) 12 App Cas 727 at 734.

interests of those in another (beneficiaries). The Christian duty of love requires trustees not to polarise issues, but to pay attention to the concerns of their beneficiaries as well as question the source of the beneficiaries' income, at the same time as pursuing a solid investment return. In terms of resolving the law's dilemma, the trustees' duty of care as it revolves around the notion of prudence could usefully be drawn more widely to take into account not just financial criteria but also other factors that inform a balanced investment strategy. True, as Sir Robert Megarry VC warned in *Cowan* v *Scargill*, 'honesty and sincerity are not the same as prudence and reasonableness',[103] and the judiciary should be careful not to sanction improvident investment activities, however honourable the motive. But, as the parable of the ten talents demonstrates, taking a Christian view on ethical investment is not automatically the antipathy of prudence or reasonableness.

Of course, broadening out the trustees' duty of care beyond the sole consideration of financial criteria will carry with it issues of weight, certainty and security. Though valid issues, these are, however, external to trustee investment, and attend any common law jurisdiction based upon judicial discretion. They are not sufficient objections *per se* to broadening out the duty of care.

Whether or not the law's dilemma over trustee ethical investments will be resolved in the proposed manner will ultimately depend upon a strong and willing judiciary, and upon continuing pressure from within and without the legal profession for law reform. While waiting for the limits of the law to be exercised, the policies now employed by trustees of church funds may be instructive to all Christian trustees in charge of other types of trusts in resolving their investment dilemmas.[104] An examination of the policies employed reveals four key features that can assist in manoeuvring around the law's environs: (1) the need for strict monitoring of investment policies and of company practices; (2) the importance of balancing interests of all parties, not least in order to secure fairness; (3) the need to foster an environment of mutual respect with the companies invested in so as to open and maintain constructive channels of communication; and (4) the recognition that whatever policy is pursued, ethical or not, it will be open to criticism.

---

[103] [1985] 1 Ch 270 at 289.
[104] See n. 68 above.

5
Can the Law Ensure Proper Stewardship of Land?

Thomas Glyn Watkin

I. Introduction

As an undergraduate at Oxford in the early 1970s, during my first term I attended a course of lectures on the Sources of Roman Law and the Roman Law of Persons. The lectures were given by a young don with a reputation for lucidity and an entertaining style, which not only guaranteed him an appreciative audience but also made him a popular after-dinner speaker at college law societies. He was known to be preparing his DPhil thesis for publication and rumour had it that his topic was the *ius stillicidii*, the Roman servitude that permitted an owner of land to allow water from his buildings to drip on to the land of a neighbour. That so interesting a teacher should be devoting a whole thesis to so narrow and apparently tedious a topic was thought, to put it mildly, curious. Rumour as ever did not contain the whole truth. When the doctoral thesis was duly published, its theme was the much broader issue of the extent to which owners in Roman law were free to do as they wished with their property and how far, if at all, they were required to respect the interests of their neighbours. The work was *Owners and Neighbours in Roman Law*.[1] Its author left academic life shortly afterwards to practise at the Scottish bar, where he has since risen to become, in fairly rapid succession, Lord Advocate, a Senator of the College of Justice and then Lord President. I refer to Lord Rodger of Earlsferry, or Alan Rodger as he appears on the title page of *Owners and Neighbours*.[2]

The thrust of Dr Rodger's thesis was an attack upon a view of ownership in Roman law that presented the concept as being absolute. The owner could do exactly as he wished with his property provided he did not interfere with the rights of others or cause them harm. He could use it, take the fruits of it and abuse it as he willed, the so-called *ius utendi, fruendi, abutendi*. The owner of a priceless work of art, for instance, was free to burn it whenever he chose; the owner of a Ming vase free to smash it without any thought for the interests of others in such a treasure of

---

[1] Oxford, Clarendon Press, 1972.
[2] Lord Rodger has since been appointed a Lord of Appeal in Ordinary (law lord).

humankind's cultural history. The owner of land was free to build some vast structure upon it provided his neighbours had no right to stop him, and such a right would require that the neighbour have a servitude for the benefit of his plot, such as a right to light or a right to stop his neighbour building or blocking his view. However unreasonable the structure, if it did not contravene some right of the neighbour's, up it could go. *Cuius est solum, eius est usque ad caelum et ad inferos* the maxim states.

So indeed states the maxim, but the maxim is not to be found in the works of Roman jurists. It first makes its appearance in the *glossa ordinaria* of the Bolognese jurist Accursius in the thirteenth century, and was imported into English law during the sixteenth century.[3] Indeed, this whole view of ownership as being absolute is a modern, not an ancient, creation. It first features as *dominium plenum* in the works of the Dutch jurist Hugo Grotius, who contrasts it with any more confined right to a thing, which he describes as *dominium minus plenum*.[4] Buttressed by the natural lawyers' subsequent development of the concept of private property as a natural right, it emerges as the untrammelled view of absolute ownership that features in the French *Code civil* of 1804 and was further developed by the Pandectist school of jurisprudence in Germany during the nineteenth century, under whose influence it came to be assumed that this was what the Roman jurists themselves had meant by *dominium*. Alan Rodger attacked that presumption.

II. Differing Views of Ownership

Lest the rather personalised perspective of my introduction be thought a self-indulgence, I should underline its importance. When we speak of the law seeking to ensure proper stewardship of land, we think of the law

[3] This late provenance has been acknowledged judicially: 'It is well known that this brocard cannot be traced in the Digest or elsewhere in Roman law. The first recognised appearance is in the 13th century gloss of the Bolognese Accursius on Digest viii.2.1 ... it only has authority at common law insofar as it has been adopted by decisions, or equivalent authority. The earliest recognition appears to be recorded in *Bury* v *Pope* [(1588) Cro Eliz at 118, sub nom *Bowry and Pope's Case* (1588) 1 Leon 168] where reference is made to its use temp Ed I ... but the context of this statement in the reign of Edward I has not been identified. Coke on Littleton 4a contains an uncritical adoption of this maxim, supported by some references (incorrect) to Year Books. He is followed by Blackstone ...'; *per* Lord Wilberforce in *Commissioner for Railways* v *Valuer-General* [1973] 3 All E.R. 268 at 277.

[4] See Hugo Grotius, *De iure belli ac pacis* 2.2. Grotius' ideas are examined in A.J. van der Walt, 'Der Eigentumsbegriff', in R. Feenstra and R. Zimmermann (eds.), *Das römisch-holländische Recht: Fortschritte des Zivilrechts im 17. und 18. Jahrhundert* (Berlin, Duncker & Humblot, 1992).

interfering with the owner's rights as owner. This in itself manifests how great the influence of the absolute concept of ownership has been in shaping modern western notions of the subject. For Grotius, *dominium plenum* entitled a man to do with a thing and for his advantage anything he pleased as long as it was not forbidden by law; *dominium plenum* allowed the owner to dispose of his property regardless of whether he was behaving like a reasonable man, a reasonable and prudent man of business or a *bonus paterfamilias*, that is according to standards the law imposes on those with a legal title less than full ownership, Grotius' *dominium minus plenum*. Ownership in this sense marked a level of personal freedom from the law's expectations with regard to the standards those in charge of property should observe and attain. Likewise, for the jurists who fashioned the absolute concept of ownership in the French *Code civil*, such ownership was a function of personal freedom, marking for them the end of the individual's subservience to feudal overlords in the management of 'his own' property.

Implicit therefore in this concept of ownership is a highly individualistic view of society. For Grotius, indeed, rights inhered in individual legal subjects, who could claim these rights either against other specific legal subjects or in relation to specific objects as against the whole world. This was to be the juristic worldview of the succeeding centuries, of the Enlightenment and of the natural law school. In a state of nature, men and women were endowed by their Creator with inalienable rights, the purpose of laws and legal systems being to maintain those rights and create the conditions within which they were capable of flourishing. The right to property was one such inalienable right, and in a state of nature there could by definition be no laws prohibiting its unrestricted exercise. Restrictions upon the freedom of owners were the work of legal orders, not of nature, and were only to be tolerated in so far as they furthered the freedom nature had given human beings. Absolute ownership was a form of liberty and was not to be enjoyed by one class only, but by all individuals equally. The cardinal principles of liberty and equality enshrined in the institutions of the American and French Revolutions combined to support the absolute idea of ownership, albeit that in practice such untrammelled power was almost certain to undermine the third cardinal virtue of the Revolution, fraternity.

Almost immediately, dissatisfaction with this absolute notion of ownership was expressed. During the early nineteenth century, the French *Code civil* was castigated as favouring the bourgeois middle classes as against the agricultural and industrial workers they employed. Capital, not labour, was thought to be protected, and a system of law beneficial to the employer and entrepreneur was believed to have been substituted for that which favoured the feudal landlord. Shortly before the outbreak of the First World War, Léon Duguit chose to deliver a course of lectures on this very theme at the University of Buenos Aires, lectures not only subsequently published in his native France but, somewhat amazingly, chosen by the American Law Schools as fundamental to understanding the development of continental law in the nineteenth century. Duguit argued that solidarity, that is fraternity expressed through the protection of the communal interest, was as essential as individual rights for the proper functioning of society.[5]

The assertion of the communal virtue of solidarity against what were seen as the excesses of individualism was more accurately the reassertion of those values. Grotius was probably the first jurist to analyse the law from the point of view of the rights and duties of individual legal subjects. His counterparts in the ancient and the medieval world did not think of *iura* as rights in that individualistic way. For the civilian and canonical jurists of previous ages, *ius* meant what was due to a particular person, connecting clearly with the justice, *iustitia*, inherent in giving a person his due, and the injustice, *iniuria*, that would result from not doing so either by withholding a benefit or inflicting some harm. The Roman jurist Ulpian summed this up in his three precepts of the law, *honeste vivere, alterum non laedere, suum cuique tribuere*.[6] To fail to act justly or to act unjustly upset the right balance of society, indeed of the world. It was to preserve this right order that people should be given their due, not because it was their natural right as individuals. Significantly, the Italian priest Antonio Rosmini redeveloped this view in the nineteenth century when he argued that law had to be based not on one's rights but upon one's respect for the rights of others.[7]

It is against this background of the preservation and development of order in the universe that St Thomas Aquinas presents his ideas with regard to private property. For St Thomas, private property is justifiable in the sense of properly accountable as due to a legal subject in that such an approach is productive of good order. People he believed were prone to look after what was theirs better than those things common to all, and allotting some things to individuals was also more productive of good order in their care and management than making everyone responsible for everything. He also believed that allowing private property decreased the opportunities for conflict over resources, which would otherwise obtain. In all of this, St Thomas is clear that whether to permit of private property or not is a matter for the state to decide; it is not a matter of natural right. While he believes on the basis of reason that it is the better option, it is neither revealed as necessary by God nor required by nature.

[5] A. Alvarez, L. Duguit et al., *The Progress of Continental Law in the Nineteenth Century* (Boston, Little, Brown, 1918; repr. New York, Rothman Reprints, 1969) [*Continental Legal History Series*, Vol. 11].
[6] See Justinian, *Institutes* 1.1.3.
[7] See A. Rosmini, *Filosofia di diritto* (Intra, 1865), esp. at 107. The work was first published in Milan in 1845, but the standard text is that published in 1865. There is an English translation of the work, entitled *Philosophy of Right*, 4 vols., tr. D. Cleary and T. Watson (Durham, Rosmini Ho., 1993).

It is because property arrangements for St Thomas are a matter of local regulation and not divine nor natural imperative that he feels able to depart from earlier traditions within the Christian community that advocated the holding of all things in common.[8] St Thomas's view was to remain standard among Catholic theologians until the time of Grotius, when the so-called Second Scholastics, such as the Spaniard Suarez, were still in substantial agreement with the Angelic Doctor. Throughout this period, the main opposition to the Thomist view came not from those arguing that property was a natural right but from those, like St Thomas's near contemporary John Duns Scotus, who held that natural law required communal, not private, ownership of property.[9]

The idea of property being a natural right took root during the seventeenth and eighteenth centuries. The English philosopher John Locke did much to advocate the notion. For him, nature required that those things with which a man mixed his labour should become his by right.[10] Private property therefore was antecedent to the social contract by which men agreed the terms upon which to found their life in society, and the terms they agreed had to uphold those rights and could not derogate from them, albeit they could regulate their enjoyment in the interests of social living. It is important to note that even for those who believed private property to be a natural right, it did not follow that there could be no restrictions upon an owner's freedom of control over his property, and clearly the social contract from which government arose was entitled to regulate the activities of owners in the interest of the collective, provided the right to property itself was not eroded.[11]

Thus it is clear that until the modern period, private property was not thought to be a natural right by Christian thinkers. Moreover, when private property came to be accounted a natural right during the seventeenth and eighteenth centuries the property rights of the owner were not thought to be unrestricted. The absolute conception of ownership

---

[8] See Acts 2:44–45.

[9] St Thomas's views can be found in his *Summa Theologica*, Part 2, Q. 66, art. 2; those of John Duns Scotus in his *Opus Oxoniense* 4.D.49, q. 4. There are valuable discussions of the changing perspectives of property and rights thereto in W. Friedman, *Legal Theory* (London, Stevens, 5th ed., 1967); and J.M. Kelly, *A Short History of Western Legal Theory* (Oxford, Clarendon Press, 1992); both *passim*.

[10] A view previously espoused by the Donatists, a heretical sect that originated at Carthage in the fourth century and whose views were severely castigated by St Augustine of Hippo. See Augustine, *Tractatus VI in Joannis Evangelium*, 25. The standard edition of Augustine's works is that by the Benedictines of St Maur (Paris, 1679–1700). This has been reprinted and is most conveniently to be found in J.-P. Migne, *Patrologia Latina* (Paris, 1841–42).

[11] John Locke, *Two Treatises on Civil Government* (London, 1690), 2, 5.

neither follows from, nor is essential to, the right to private property, whether that right is accounted part of the natural order or not. Further, there are some who have argued that although property is a natural right, it does not obtain for the benefit of individuals but for society. Property exists for the common good. On this, the Scholastic proponents of private property would be at one with those who maintained the propriety of a community of goods.

Writing of the concept of ownership in the 1960s, A.M. Honoré chose to describe ownership as the 'greatest possible interest in a thing which a mature system of law recognizes'. The working definition provided by Honoré harks back to Grotius' *dominium plenum* but differs from it in that it is not absolute. For Honoré, a mature legal system may stop short of allowing an interest so great as to be termed absolute. Honoré went on to delineate ten standard incidents of this concept. These are a right to possess the thing, a right to use it, a right to manage it, and a right to take its income, which amount in effect to the *ius utendi et fruendi* mentioned earlier. Fifthly, there is the right to the capital, allowing for alienation, consumption, waste or destruction in whole or in part. This is the *ius abutendi*, and while Honoré admits that it may not go unrestricted in a mature legal system, he also believes that its absence would negative the idea of ownership. Honoré also regards the right to security as being a standard incident: that an owner expects to be safe in the knowledge that his ownership is protected against all-comers. At this point, Honoré's idea of ownership can no longer be a natural phenomenon but must be a social construct; only through the existence of law within a legal order can such security be enjoyed. The other standard incidents Honoré describes are the incident of transmissibility, the incident of absence of term and finally the two very significant ones of prohibition of harmful use and liability to execution, for instance in satisfaction of debts, with Honoré adding that a good case could also be made for including liability to tax and to expropriation by the state. Again, in relation to the incident of execution in all or any of its forms, a concept of ownership which has these as standard incidents owes something to the imposition of legal order and cannot be simply the manifestation of a natural right. Interestingly, by the middle years of the twentieth century, a legal scholar's concept of ownership places him closer to the tradition of St Thomas Aquinas than that of his chronologically nearer forerunners in the natural law and Pandectist schools.[12]

The concept of ownership therefore is not static; it is affected by the prevailing intellectual climate and has indeed undergone extensive change over time. The understanding of one generation regarding its meaning may be far removed from that of its immediate predecessors, and may be far closer to that of more remote times. It is therefore pertinent to

---

[12] A.M. Honoré, 'Ownership', in A.G. Guest (ed.), *Oxford Essays in Jurisprudence* (Oxford, Clarendon Press, 1961), 107–147.

inquire what, in Honoré's phrase, mature legal systems have in the past accounted to be ownership and to what extent their notion of ownership has been structured in the interests of stewardship. This is important as the modern concept of ownership is the result of the gradual development of the concept in Europe.

III. Ownership in Past Ages

Roman law placed things, *res*, into two broad categories according to whether or not they were permitted to be privately owned. Those susceptible of private ownership were called *res in commercio*; those a private person could not own were termed *res extra commercium*. The things that could not be owned privately were in part things devoted to the gods, such as temples and sacred groves, and in the Christian era churches, in part those devoted to the spirits of the dead, such as graves, tombs and monuments, and those things under the special protection of the gods because of their strategic importance – city walls, gates and the like. These three categories – *res sacrae, religiosae* and *sanctae* respectively were *res divini iuris*, under divine law, and therefore incapable of human ownership. There were also however things under human law, *res humani iuris*, but which could not be privately owned, namely those things common to all, such as the air, the sea and the seashore, those things common to all citizens of a state, such as navigable rivers, ports and highways, and those common to all the inhabitants of a community, such as its market places, theatres, baths and other public amenities. So, one could not in Roman law acquire title to a temple by purchase or assert a title by long possession of a part of the seashore.[13]

Roman private law ownership, *dominium*, did not therefore extend to such things. In strict theory also, provincial land – whether in senatorial or imperial provinces – was incapable of being privately owned, although those who were entitled to the possession of such land were to all intents and purposes owners, in much the same way as the English tenant in fee simple absolute in possession is accounted virtual owner of the land and not just of his estate. Land in Italy on the other hand, as opposed to land in the provinces, was capable of private ownership. This is what was meant by Italic land, land south of the River Po, which was one of the four heads of private property in Roman law, the so-called *res mancipi*, which

---

[13] See Gaius, *Institutes* 2.1–11; Justinian, *Institutes* 2.1. pr-11; Digest 1.8. Convenient editions of these texts with an English translation are: *The Institutes of Gaius*, ed. F. de Zulueta (Oxford, Clarendon Press, 1946); *The Institutes of Gaius*, ed. W.M. Gordon and O.F. Robinson (London, Duckworth, 1988); *Justinian's Institutes*, ed. P. Birks and G. McLeod (London, Duckworth, 1987); Digest, ed. T. Mommsen, P. Krueger and A. Watson (Philadelphia, University of Pennsylvania Press, 1985).

required strict formalities for conveyance of legal title, *dominium*. The other heads were slaves, beasts of draft and burden and certain easements, namely rights of way over a neighbour's land on foot, with animals or in a vehicle, and the right to draw water over the land of another. Modern scholarship however holds that Italic land was the last of the four items to be included in this list of *res mancipi*, and that because originally, in archaic Rome, land had not been capable of being privately owned.[14]

This view holds considerable interest. It postulates a Rome similar to many other early societies, including Canaan at the time of its occupation by the children of Israel[15] and also rural England in the medieval period. Early Rome, it would appear, consisted of city dwellings surrounded by common fields, rather like the common fields of the Middle Ages. Periodically, the fields would be allotted among the families for their use and cultivation, but only for a fixed length of time. From time to time, the land would be redistributed, among other things to ensure that families with few descendants did not prosper at the expense of those with many through the retention of more land than they needed. Interestingly, this means that rights of way and so on over land were capable of existing and being owned ahead of the land itself over which those rights were exercised.[16] No substantial evidence of the legal arrangements relating to this phase of Roman agricultural and legal development survives. It is not known what standards, if any, the allotment holders were expected to attain, but there may be some vestiges of them in later legal arrangements concerning the management of land and other property.[17]

Most notably perhaps this may be the case in relation to the well-known Roman legal institution according to a person rights less than full *dominium*, namely the usufruct. The usufruct gave the

---

[14] That this was the case is suggested by Varro's account of the allotments made by Romulus: see Varro, *De re rustica* 1.10.A; a convenient edition with English translation is that in the Loeb Library, No. 283 (London, Heinemann, 1935).

[15] When agricultural land was not freely alienable. A distinction was drawn between urban and rural properties, the former being capable of transfer by sale in perpetuity, the latter not, being the allotment given to a particular family; see Lev. 25:29–34. This raises an interesting comparison with the Roman distinction with regard to rights over the land of others, which were grouped as either rustic or urban praedial servitudes. See, for instance, Gaius, *Institutes* 2.14; Justinian *Institutes* 2.3.

[16] Varro, *De re rustica* 1.10. The issue is discussed in T.G. Watkin, *An Historical Introduction to Modern Civil Law* (Aldershot, Dartmouth, 1999), at 256–258.

[17] Later arrangements, with some attention to history, are described in Cato, *De agri cultura*, and Varro, *De re rustica*. The text of Cato's work, with an English translation is to be found in No. 283 of the Loeb Library (London, Heinemann, 1935).

usufructuary the right to use and enjoy property, for our purposes land, provided that the substance of the property was not affected, *salva rerum substantia*. In other words, the property was not to be exploited in a manner that diminished its value. Thus the usufructuary had to farm the land, occupy the house or treat the animals in a way that did not diminish the capital value of the goods. If the land already had a quarry on it or had been used for mining, the usufructuary could pursue those activities, but he could not open a quarry or sink a mine on land that had not previously been put to such use. In his management of the property, he was expected to observe the standards of a good head of family, a *bonus paterfamilias*, the reasonable and prudent man – or, perhaps more accurately, manager – of Roman legal parlance.[18]

The interesting question for our purposes is whether this standard, in classical Roman law applied to the usufructuary among a range of other users, possessors and borrowers of things, was ever applied or thought to apply generally to the full owner, the *dominus* himself. The absolute view of Roman ownership cultivated by the conceptual analysis of the Pandectists would pour scorn on this suggestion. Such scorn may be misplaced, for there is evidence to support the view that the *dominus* himself may not have had a free hand to abuse his property. To begin with, he was not free to dispose of it as he wished upon his death. Those who were regarded as being his heirs as of right, namely the children in his power (*potestas*), could not be disinherited other than for good cause. If they were, they could upset such a will. Moreover, it came to be recognised that each such heir was entitled to a fixed portion of the inheritance, as was the heir appointed by will, so that if less were received, all other legacies and gifts could be scaled down to restore to the heirs their share.[19]

Nor was the Roman owner able to circumvent these rules by making gifts during his lifetime. Although the head of the family, the *paterfamilias*, was the only member of the family with property rights, the future expectations of his children were not unprotected. If the *pater* began to dispose of what was legally his property in a prodigal manner, a curator could be appointed to manage the property in his stead, the institution known as *cura prodigi*, the guardianship of spendthrifts. A similar guardianship, the *cura furiosi*, existed in relation to the insane, in order to protect the expectations of the next of kin and, interestingly, if they were disinherited unjustly in a will, the testator was for that reason alone deemed to have been insane. Thus, within the family unit, so important within Roman society, the *paterfamilias* as *dominus* was far from having a free

---

[18] On the usufruct, see W.W. Buckland, *A Textbook of Roman Law*, revised by P.G. Stein (Cambridge, Cambridge University Press, 3rd ed., 1963), 269–273.

[19] The *querela inofficiosi testamenti* and the Falcidian quarter respectively. For details see Buckland, *Textbook*, 327–332, 342–343.

hand to do as he wished with his property.[20] According to Honoré's standard incidents, the Roman owner was markedly short on having a right to the capital; he could certainly not waste or destroy his property, and his family may well have been able to police his ability to alienate and consume.[21] In short, here may lie the roots of the concept of the *bonus paterfamilias* to be applied widely as a standard of conduct and care in Roman law.

The concept of the Roman *dominus* as an absolute owner relied more however upon his freedom with regard to his neighbours, and it was this aspect of the absolute view that Alan Rodger attacked. The Pandectist approach postulated an owner of land who could do whatever he liked on his property provided he did not actually injure,[22] that is harm, the person or property of others. If his activities did not cause legally redressable injury, then the only circumstance in which a neighbouring owner could legitimately interfere would be where he had a right, that is a servitude, over the offender's land entitling him to restrict what would otherwise be lawful activities.

One anomaly however appeared to exist. The Roman law of servitudes knew of a right to build upon one's land, the *ius altius tollendi*, and the right to prevent one's neighbour building, the *ius altius non tollendi*. As a matter of logic, either an owner could build on his land or not, so that it would appear that either the owner of land must have the *ius altius tollendi* or his neighbour the *ius altius non tollendi*. The servitudes appear to be logical contradictories; one or the other must exist, nothing else is possible. Such a situation would nevertheless be strange in that servitudes burden one parcel of land for the benefit of another; the owner who may build higher burdens his neighbour with having to suffer the consequences; the owner who may not build higher is burdened by the neighbour's right to restrain what should otherwise be lawful activity. The problem with treating the servitudes as logical contradictories is that servitudes are meant to permit what would otherwise be unlawful, but there is nothing left in the middle that could be lawful if one or the other must exist. It would appear to be unlawful to build and unlawful to prevent one's neighbour building.

---

[20] For these institutions of *cura*, see *ibid*. 168–169.

[21] The literal contract of early Roman law may provide evidence of how this was done. The contract relied on each head of household keeping strict accounts in a ledger, the entries in which could have provided evidence of prodigality and indeed even of insanity. For further details of the contract, see *ibid*. 459–461.

[22] This approach is best exemplified by B. Windscheid, *Lehrbuch des Pandektenrechts* (Frankfurt-am-Main, Rütten & Leoning, 9th ed., 1906), Vol. 1, §167 at 857. The Pandectist approach was severely criticised by Gierke; see O. von Gierke, *Der Entwurf eines burgerlichen Gesetzbuch und das deutsche Recht* (Leipzig, Duncker & Humblot, rev. ed., 1889), 103, 323.

Rodger exposed this anomaly and suggested a much more satisfactory interpretation. Both the *ius altius tollendi* and the *ius altius non tollendi* he proposed allowed conduct that exceeded what was otherwise lawful. In other words, the *ius altius tollendi* allowed an owner to build higher than would otherwise be permitted by law. Likewise, the *ius altius non tollendi* allowed a neighbour to veto any building by the adjacent owner even to an extent that was otherwise not unlawful. The norm, the middle ground as it were, consisted of owners being allowed to build on their land to an extent that was not unreasonable. To exceed that limit needed a servitude – the *ius altius tollendi* – as did any restriction upon a neighbour's right to build reasonably – the *ius altius non tollendi*. According to Rodger, therefore, Roman owners had no absolute right to do as they wished with their own. Such extreme power required rights in excess of normal ownership, even though no legal injury to the property of the other might result. *Dominium* was a limited set of rights.[23]

It can therefore be seen that both with regard to neighbours and to future generations, a Roman owner was expected to show forbearance. His control of his property was not unrestricted, but subject to limitations set not just by the rights of others but by their expectations and interests, and this despite the fact that the right of ownership was vested in an individual legal person.

The Germanic tribes who succeeded to the lands of the western Roman empire in the wake of its gradual abandonment by the Romans did not regard land ownership as being fundamentally an individual matter. For them, land was vested either in a family or a clan or in the community. Ownership of land was therefore necessarily limited, in the sense that the individual head of household, the *Hausherr*, was required to recognise the interests of others in property in which as yet they had no rights, whether subsequent generations of his family or the wider community if he had no descendants. The same was true of lands that villagers brought into cultivation outside their previous boundaries, the land of the *Mark*, or March. In such areas, the *Mark* community exercised a form of communal ownership that, unlike the partnerships – *societates* – of Roman law, was not based upon contractual relationships among the partners. This was one of the great differences between the Roman and Germanic traditions; Roman law saw property rights as vested in individuals, whereas Germanic law allowed for corporate ownership and group personality. Although at the Reception the civilian jurists attempted to encompass the Germanic notions within the familiar contractual categories of Roman learning, they were ultimately

---

[23] See Rodger, *Owners and Neighbours*, ch. 1. In subsequent chapters the argument is pursued in an analysis of other servitudes concerning the right to light (ch. 2), the right of prospect (ch. 4) and rights with regard to water (ch. 5). Chapter 3 on remedies developed the argument relating to the *ius altius tollendi*.

unsuccessful, for the Germanic concepts, like new wine in old bottles, burst forth to contribute the concepts of corporation and communal ownership to modern civilian jurisprudence.[24]

Between the age of the Germanic tribes and the revival and Reception of Roman law lie the centuries of feudalism, and feudalism also stands in opposition to the idea of absolute ownership. In the wake of the demise of the Carolingian empire, the proprietors of land surrendered their estates to powerful lords in return for their protection. These lords granted the lands to their erstwhile owners in return for their promise of loyalty and service. Such feudal compacts were in the bone contractual arrangements, but the tenants were given their lands for life, or even on terms that allowed their heirs to succeed on their death. Nevertheless, the lord retained an interest and a control over his tenants' activities. At times, such control extended to licensing alienations, ensuring that the land was not overexploited to the detriment of its future yield and seeing that the tenants' heirs were suitably trained to become good tenants in their turn.[25] This is indeed a far cry from the absolute conception of the owner's powers advocated in the seventeenth and eighteenth centuries very much as a reaction against the constraints of feudal overlordship. Civilian jurisprudence found it difficult to discern who between lords and tenants was the owner, and made use of a variety of Roman concepts, some of which they developed ingeniously, to resolve the difficulties.[26] The reality of feudal land tenure was however that the interests of a range of persons, from the ruler at the top of the feudal ladder through a number of intermediate or mesne lords to the tenant in actual possession at the bottom, were recognised as having interests in the one property, which militated against anyone having a complete right to do with the land entirely as he or she wished.

---

[24] See Watkin, *Historical Introduction*, 225–226.

[25] *Ibid.* 221–223.

[26] The distinction between *Dominium directum* and *dominium utile* was based upon a distinction in classical Roman law between actions. Whereas an owner could bring a direct action, *actio directa*, to recover his property, a non-owner with an interest in the property could not use the owner's remedy because his interest was less than ownership. Accordingly, the praetor gave him an action based upon that of the owner, an *actio utilis*, to recover the thing. Following the Roman jurists, the medieval civilians were not prepared to accept that there could be different levels of ownership; therefore the interests of the tenant and the lord in the same parcel of land were regarded as similar to that of the owner and a person having rights less than full ownership respectively, the lord's interest being regarded as limited to his services. Therefore, by analogy with the Roman distinction, the tenant in demesne was regarded as having the direct ownership, *dominium directum*, while the lord's interest in the services was described as *dominium utile*. See further Watkin, *Historical Introduction*, 227–228.

Feudalism wrought a further significant change upon the Roman understanding of ownership. Whereas Roman law had been prepared to accept that certain things were not capable of being owned in private law, feudalism's conjunction of political power and property, *imperium* and *dominium*, jurisdiction and ownership, in the person of the lord led to a refusal to accept that anything could lie outside of the lord's protection and therefore, in a sense, his property. Those things therefore that Roman law had said were *extra commercium*, feudalism placed under the special protection of the lord – highways, navigable rivers, the seashore, market places and other open spaces, which the public were entitled to frequent and use, such as common land, open forests and the like.[27] Feudalism's abhorrence of a vacuum with regard to the ownership of property also led it to reject the notion of things capable of being owned being at any time without an owner, Roman law's *res nullius*. Thus abandoned goods passed to the lord as did the property of those who died leaving no one to inherit, *bona vacantia*. Likewise, wild animals in Roman law had belonged to no one until they were captured, but the feudal principle demanded that they be the property of someone, so that they were accounted the property of the landowner upon whose land they were to be found. This led to game in the forests being accounted the special property of the lord, laying the foundation for the stern game and forest laws that were a feature of the Middle Ages. Hunting in the forest and fishing in the rivers were accounted aristocratic pursuits, which the ordinary person could only undertake with the express permission of the lord under whose protection the land or waterway subsisted. Gradually, almost inevitably, the lord's protection became indistinguishable from his ownership, although the original idea had been that he should exercise a police power over the activities of the hunters and fishermen in the interests of maintaining the common interest in the stock and terrain.

With the advent of the absolute idea of ownership, such feudal arrangements with regard to hunting and fishing underwent two developments. Firstly, lords, believing themselves to be the true owners of such property rather than its protectors or stewards, no longer felt obligated to permit their tenants to hunt and fish on the land. Accordingly, much common land came to be enclosed, no longer available to the ordinary person for recreation or pasture. Only if a right to do so could be established would such practices need to be permitted. This made for great inequality with regard to the amenities of land ownership. Secondly, and partly as a result of the first development, with the French Revolution, liberty and equality were asserted with regard to the perceived common right to hunt and fish. Thus, in the French *Code civil* and later codifications which followed the French example, landowners

---

[27] The emperor's claims had been fully set out at the Diet of Roncaglia in 1158; see Watkin, *Historical Introduction*, 222–223.

are again obligated, in true Roman style, to allow anyone who so wishes to hunt and fish on their lands provided they do no damage and that the landowner is not prosecuting a particularly sensitive activity thereon that justifies his exclusion of strangers.[28] This does not permit the public to resort to private estates for the pursuit of other leisure activities such as walking, picnicking or rambling. Indeed, across continental Europe the somewhat odd principle holds that one may only enter upon a neighbour's land uninvited if one is armed with a gun.[29]

If the enclosures of the seventeenth and eighteenth century marked the zenith of lordly ownership and the unrestricted liberty and equality of every owner the apogee of the absolute conception of *dominium*, neither left much room for ownership as stewardship for the communal benefit, which was both St Thomas Aquinas's justification for permitting private property and can in many ways be said to be more representative of what the concept of ownership has been intended to supply during the greater part of human social and legal history. Nevertheless, what may be termed the modern concept of ownership, in common law and civilian jurisdictions, owes much to the absolute theory of the Pandectists and of the French *Code civil*. In part this may be attributed to the fact that this view coincided with and assisted the making of large, sometimes vast, personal fortunes by individual industrialists and men of commerce, which they felt they had made for themselves and should therefore be free to dispose of as they pleased. By and large, the responses to this phenomenon in terms of attempts to confine its worst tendencies and features belong in the realm of public rather than private law.

IV. Modern Restrictions on Ownership

The concept of the complete freedom of an owner to do as he wishes with his property in private law has led to restrictions being placed upon owners in public law, thus neatly leaving untouched the theoretically absolute nature of ownership as a matter of private law.[30] Modern states have circumscribed the rights of owners to alter the use to which their property is put, to improve it, to build upon it, to extend buildings upon it, to undertake industrial practices upon it, all in the name of ensuring

---

[28] *Code civil*, art. 715; and since 1955 (*Loi 16 avril*) *Code rural*, art. 366. The clearest example is probably that of Italy, *Codice civile*, art. 842 and 923.

[29] For Spain, for instance, see *Código civil*, art. 611; *Ley de Caza* 4 *abril* 1970 and *Regl. 25 marzo* 1971; *Ley de Pesca Fluvial* 20 feb. 1942.

[30] In England and Wales, for example, it was not until 1909 that local authorities were given general powers to control development of land in the Housing, Town Planning, etc., Act of that year. Subsequent statutes extended this control culminating in the Town and Country Planning Act 1932, which significantly extended control to rural as well as urban land.

that the common interest in the maintenance of a neighbourhood is not undermined by an individual owner's exercise of his private law powers. Not only are innovations controlled; periodically, as the demands of a healthier, even more attractive, environment are recognised and adopted, existing activities are on occasion subjected to more stringent regulation in the interest of ensuring that the environment and the heritage are protected.

Such public law intrusion into the close of the private law owner might well be accounted by some a trespass. Indeed, in most jurisdictions it has come to be regulated by a new department of public law commonly called administrative law in deference to the highly developed and highly regarded *droit administratif* that has grown up in France since the first half of the nineteenth century. It is not too much to say that this area of law bears testimony to the manner in which public law has had to regulate private law rights in order to redress the imbalance caused by the absolute concept of ownership, which reached a high water mark in the *Code civil*.

The *droit administratif* of France has however pioneered a significant development with regard to administrative and legislative decisions that adversely affect the existing rights of owners, namely they may only be carried into effect upon compensation being paid by the administrative body or the state to the private persons affected.[31] The Common Agricultural Policy of the European Community is arguably a recognition of this principle writ large. Administrative law in several jurisdictions has recognised that those who may be adversely affected by an administrative decision relating to an owner's application for planning permission, for instance, have a right to be heard before such an application is determined.[32] In Italy, the juristic doctrine has gone further and recognised that such rights exist to protect legitimate interests regarding the

---

[31] This development has occurred as a result of the *Conseil d'État* constructing a principle of liability without fault based upon the theory of risk. It recognises that state activities, even when faultless, can place citizens' rights at risk. It has also been referred, and that most significantly for the argument advanced here, to the principle of the equality of all citizens in bearing public burdens and therefore the injustice of allowing any loss arising from public acts to rest upon individual citizens, a view expressed most forcefully by Léon Duguit in his *Traité de Droit Constitutionnel* (Paris, Ancienne Librarie Fontemoing, 3rd ed., 1927–29), at 469. For a full discussion of the issue, see J.S. Bell and L.N. Brown, *French Administrative Law* (Oxford, Clarendon Press, 1998).

[32] In England and Wales, for instance, such provisions are contained in the Town and Country Planning Act 1990, ss. 16, 20, 42 and 79. The juridical nature of such rights in England and Wales is discussed in David Harte, 'A Christian Approach to Environmental Law?' in Paul R. Beaumont (ed.), *Christian Perspectives on Law Reform* (Carlisle, Paternoster, 1998).

environment, the neighbourhood and other such personal interests in the community, which interests are antecedent to and exist independently of the law's protection. One might almost say that they are natural interests arising from natural rights that exist in community rather than in individuality.[33]

An example at this point may assist. The Roman lawyers listed among those things not susceptible of private ownership the air we breathe.[34] This may appear to be so obvious as not to need stating, indeed as a positively otiose statement. However, in that air cannot be individually owned, it follows that no individual has rights in it, and therefore if someone pollutes the air, although this offends others, no one can thereby complain of having suffered damage or an injury. Only if an individual's person or property is harmed can a complaint be brought for redress; only if such a harm is anticipated can such a pollution be forbidden. However, in that the air is common to all humankind, everyone has an interest in its purity. Accordingly, the community is entitled to regulate emissions and any other activities that might cause pollution in order to protect the common legitimate interest; indeed, it can be argued that there is a duty upon the community to do so, otherwise the legitimate interest each person severally has in the air he or she shares with the rest of humanity may be adversely affected by someone else's poor stewardship of that resource.

The advent of public law methods of restricting the excesses of owners has left unaffected the private law remedies of neighbours. A neighbour is still able to confine the activities of an owner by agreeing with him to burden his land with a servitude, an easement or, in English law, a restrictive covenant.[35] Even without such substantive rights, an owner may still find himself liable to a neighbour for any activity undertaken on his property that consequentially harms his neighbour, although he may in such circumstances be able to raise the defence of justification, that is, having a legal right to prosecute the harmful activity. Even where such a right exists, some legal systems have restricted the lawfulness of its exercise by insisting that a consequentially harmful activity can only be carried on where the intention is to benefit the owner. If the intention is to harm or annoy the neighbour, the otherwise lawful nature of the activity ceases to justify it. This inroad into an

---

[33] For further details see T.G. Watkin, *The Italian Legal Tradition* (Aldershot, Ashgate, 1997), 146–156.

[34] See Justinian, *Institutes* 2.1.1.

[35] 'Servitude' is the term usually employed in civilian jurisdictions: for France, see *Code civil*, art. 637–710; for Italy, *Codice civile*, art. 1027–1099; for Spain, *Código civil*, art. 530–604. In common law jurisdictions, the word 'easement' is more frequently employed, as for instance in England and Wales. Easements and restrictive covenants are today Class D charges on land under the Land Charges Act 1925, s. 10.

owner's freedom is described in Scots law as *aemulatio vicini*, a concept derived from Roman law where its focus was rivalry between neighbouring towns rather than properties, and in French law the concept has been developed under the title of abuse of rights.[36] Exercising a right purely to cause loss to another renders its exercise unlawful. Indeed, some writers suggest that the absence of benefit to the owner is in itself evidence of ill will and of an abuse of rights. One French commentator, Josserand, has gone as far as to suggest that owners' rights in this regard can only lawfully be exercised for the social purpose they were intended by the law to further, all such rights being intended to further the common and not just the individual good.[37] Here one sees once more a reaction to the absolutist view of ownership engendered by the *Code civil* as well as a distinct echo of St Thomas Aquinas's justification for the existence of private property. English law differentiates activities that adversely affect the reasonable use and enjoyment of specific neighbours from those that affect the public at large in its distinction between private and public nuisance, the latter being a crime for which individuals who are particularly prejudiced may bring a civil action for redress.[38]

V. What are the Limits of the Law in this Regard?

This somewhat lengthy consideration of the meaning of ownership has served to emphasise two important points. Firstly, not all thinkers agree that private property is a natural right as opposed to one justified within the regulation of a particular society as being for the common good. Secondly, the concept of ownership is not necessarily synonymous with the kind of *dominium* recognised and upheld by the *Code civil* and by various nineteenth-century views of private property. Instead, through most of the history of western law, in both the common law and civil law families, the accepted concept of ownership has involved restrictions placed upon the owner for the benefit of others, sometimes future generations of his own family, sometimes neighbours or the wider community. In short, there should be no embarrassment in suggesting that restrictions upon the powers of owners should be imposed for the good of the wider

---

[36] See David Johnston 'Owners and Neighbours: From Rome to Scotland', in R. Evans-Jones (ed.), *The Civil Law Tradition in Scotland* (Edinburgh, Stair Society, 1995), 176–197; *Amos and Walton's Introduction to French Law*, 3rd ed., by F.H. Lawson, A.E. Anton and L. Neville Brown (Oxford, Clarendon Press, 1967), 219–220; E. Reid, 'Abuse of Rights in Scots Law' (1998) 2 *Edinburgh Law Review* 129–157.

[37] L. Josserand, *De l'esprit des droits et de leur relativité* (Paris, Dalloz, 1927; 1939), no. 292.

[38] For a recent discussion of developments in English and Scots law, see, E. Reid, 'EastEnders and Neighbours' (1998) 2 *Edinburgh Law Review* 94–100.

community. Such has been the rule rather than the exception in most countries in most ages and is arguably necessary to fulfil the underlying purpose of private ownership as a permissible legal institution, even if property is regarded as a natural right.[39]

The foregoing discussion has also indicated a number of different methods of controlling the excesses of private owners. Virtually every legal system has mechanisms by which neighbours and other third parties may obtain redress for harms caused by an owner in the exercise of his rights or for interference with the rights of others. In ensuring that owners comply with the required standards in such circumstances, such private law methods leave something to be desired in terms of efficiency. While one has no reason to suspect that the vast majority of owners will and do respect the interests of others in the manner in which they exercise their rights and powers, those who overstep the mark will only be brought to book if the third party affected chooses to pursue the matter and seek a declaration of their rights or some form of redress, and in the past it has sometimes proved difficult for remedies to be obtained by the weak and poor when the offenders were powerful.[40] There is also the problem that in today's world the damage suffered may be wide and its seriousness such that *ex post facto* awards of damages cannot provide adequate compensation. The preferred alternative is, and has been for almost two centuries, the imposition of public law controls upon owners to ensure that the worst excesses of individual action are avoided rather than cured.

There is therefore little doubt that the law can ensure that certain standards are observed in the management of land in private ownership. The law of nuisance entails that owners can be expected to measure up to the standard of the reasonable man in those of their activities that could be harmful to others. The development of the standard of the reasonable and prudent man of business in relation to trustees and other fiduciaries provides a further standard relating to management achievement among those who act for the benefit of others. Indeed, it is worth remembering that the equitable concept of the fiduciary relationship began as the imposition of obligations upon those who were legal

---

[39] For a recent discussion of the options open to the legislator, see D.W. McKenzie Skene, J. Rowan-Robinson, R. Paisley and D.J. Cusine, 'Stewardship: From Rhetoric to Reality' (1999) 3 *Edinburgh Law Review* 151–175. For a more extended treatment of the changing concept of ownership from Roman times to the present, see T.G. Watkin, 'Ownership in Public and Private Law' (1999) 11 *Sri Lanka Journal of International Law* 251–276.

[40] This was characterised as the problem of the 'overmighty subject' in the fifteenth and sixteenth centuries, when the prerogative courts, such as that of Star Chamber, sought to restrain by royal authority the worst excesses of such men and institutions.

owners, but who, in conscience, a key element in the medieval origins of the equitable jurisdiction and the importance of which has been reiterated recently by the House of Lords,[41] had to exercise their powers of ownership in the interests of others and eventually according to the aforementioned standards. Likewise, the civil law's *bonus paterfamilias*, reincarnated in the *bon père de la famille*, the *buon padre di famiglia* and the *buen padre de familia* of the modern French, Italian and Spanish codes exemplifies further evidence of standards of stewardship being imposed upon those with some of the rights of owners for the benefit of others with rights or interests in the object of ownership concerned.[42] The *bonus paterfamilas* and the reasonable and prudent man of business are both exemplars of a standard of stewardship perceived to be desirable in certain societies. Two questions remain to be addressed. What is the appropriate standard to be expected in a Christian community, and can such a standard be ensured?

VI. Christian Stewardship of the Land

According to the first account of the creation of man in Genesis, God made man in his own image and after his own likeness, and gave him *dominion* over the fish of the sea, the fowl of the air, over cattle and creeping things and over all the earth. At the time of their creation, humans were blessed by God and told to be fruitful, to multiply, to replenish the earth and subdue it and to have *dominion* over all living creatures.[43]

Man's place in the created order is special because he is made in the image and likeness of God. Some see in the words 'image and likeness' an example of that parallelism of expression so valued in Hebrew literature. Others however regard the words as having distinct meanings, *image* referring to the qualities of reason and free will with which humans are endowed by God, while *likeness* is taken to refer to supernatural attributes, the so-called *donum superadditum*, lost as a result of the fall but manifest in the perfect humanity of Christ and available to his followers through faith in him and the regenerative power of the Holy Spirit. Interpretations of the effect of the fall upon man as *imago Dei* (as opposed to man as *similitudo Dei*) vary; some, like Luther, see the image as having been lost; others, like Calvin, account it corrupted but not entirely forfeit. Catholic theologians regard reason, for instance, as having

---

[41] See *Westdeutsche Landesbank Girozentrale* v *Islington London Borough Council* [1996] A.C. 669; esp. the speech of Lord Browne-Wilkinson.

[42] For the application of this standard in relation to the usufruct, see for ancient Rome, Justinian, *Institutes* 2.1.38; for France, *Code civil*, art. 601; for Spain, *Código civil*, art. 497; for Italy, *Codice civile*, art. 1001.

[43] Gen. 1:26.

become fallible by virtue of the fall, but nevertheless regard it as reliable in so far as it is not at odds with divine revelation.[44]

The dominion humans are granted by God over the created order has been interpreted, rather like ownership or *dominium*, differently in different ages. Unsurprisingly, during the seventeenth, eighteenth and nineteenth centuries, when the absolute conception of ownership grew in influence and held sway, the created order was viewed functionally, existing for humanity's benefit and free to be exploited by us. Although such an approach can be detected in the thinking of Origen in the early church[45] and in the writings of Peter Lombard,[46] Thomas Aquinas[47] and John Calvin,[48] it reaches its apogee with thinkers such as Francis Bacon[49] and René Descartes.[50] Against that approach, there stands a tradition more closely associated with the Orthodox East than the Catholic West, which regards humanity's dominion as being a trusteeship or stewardship of creation, to be exercised in a Godlike manner, that is, in accordance with Christ's precept to be as one who serves.[51] This view can be seen in the teachings of St Basil the Great,[52] St John Chrysostom,[53]

[44] See James F. Childress, 'Image of God *(Imago Dei)*, in J. Macquarrie and J. Childress (eds.), *A New Dictionary of Christian Ethics* (London, SCM, 1986).

[45] See Origen, *Exhortation to Martyrdom*, 34 ff., a convenient English version to be found in *Alexandrian Christianity*, ed. J.E.L. Oulton and H. Chadwick (London, SCM Press, 1954) [*Library of Christian Classics*]; *De Principis* IX, ed. A. Roberts and J. Donaldson (Peabody, Mass., 1994; a reprint of *Ante-Nicene Fathers*, Vol. 4, first published Edinburgh, T. & T. Clark, 1885).

[46] In, for instance, his Commentaries on the Psalms, which can most conveniently be found in the collection of his *Opera* in *Patrologia Latina*, ed. J.-P. Migne (Paris, 1879–80), 191–192.

[47] *Summa Theologica* 1a, Q. 22, ed. A.M. Fairweather (London, SCM Press, 1954) [*Library of Christian Classics*].

[48] *Institutes of the Christian Religion* 1.5.16 and 18, ed. J.T. McNeill and F.L. Battles (London, SCM Press, 1961) [*Library of Christian Classics*].

[49] *The Works of Francis Bacon*, ed. J. Spedding, R.L. Ellis and D.D. Heath (London, Longman, 1857–59), Vol. 6, at 747.

[50] See *Le Monde* (Paris, 1664), a convenient English translation to be found in *Descartes: The World and Other Writings*, ed. S. Gaukroger (Cambridge, Cambridge University Press, 1998).

[51] See Terence R. Anderson, 'Environmental Ethics', in Macquarrie and Childress, *New Dictionary of Christian Ethics*; R. Attfield, *The Ethics of Environmental Concern* (Oxford, Blackwell, 1983).

[52] Basil of Caesarea, *The Hexaemeron*, ed. B. Jackson (Peabody, Mass., Hendrickson, 1994; a reprint of *Nicene and Post-Nicene Fathers*: 2nd Series, Vol. 8, first published 1895).

[53] Homilies 3, 4 and 26, ed. P. Schaff (Peabody, Mass., Hendrickson, 1994; a reprint of *Nicene and Post-Nicene Fathers*: 1st Series, Vol. 14, first published 1889).

St Augustine[54] and St Francis of Assisi,[55] and has exercised a powerful influence on a range of twentieth-century Christian thinkers.[56] Man must project the image of God within Creation, exercising his Godlike qualities of reason and free will to serve the whole created order, which owes its being to the work of God as creator and sustainer. This humans are enabled to do by faith in the redemption God has wrought in Christ and through the regenerative power of the Holy Spirit. Creation is seen in one of two ways. Firstly, as having an instrumental value for human life and well-being, and not only that of the present generation but also of future generations who are part of the moral community, the well-being of which the present generation must respect in its activities. Alternatively, for some the created order itself stands redeemed and is of intrinsic rather than instrumental worth and therefore to be guarded by us in accordance with God's purpose both for humankind and for the created universe.[57]

There is thus much dispute concerning the meaning of stewardship as regards the meaning of ownership. If creation is viewed instrumentally, the dominical instruction to take no thought for the morrow[58] sits

---

[54] *Exposition of the Literal Meaning of Genesis* and *Exposition of the Psalms: Psalm VII*, ed. A.C. Coxe (Peabody, Mass., Hendrickson, 1994; a reprint of *Nicene and Post-Nicene Fathers*: 1st Series, Vol. 8, first published 1888).

[55] Most notably in his *Canticle of Brother Sun*, a convenient English version of which can be found in *Francis and Clare: The Complete Works*, ed. R.J. Armstrong and I.C. Brady (London, SPCK, 1982), at 37.

[56] For example, Jürgen Moltmann, *God in Creation* (London, SCM, 1985); L. Newbigin, *The Other Side of 1984* (London, British Council of Churches, 1983); and numerous reports by the churches, including: Church of England Board for Social Responsibility, *Our Responsibility for the Living Environment* (London, Church House, 1986); Church of Scotland Science, Religion and Technology Project, *While the Earth Endures* (Edinburgh, Quorum Press, 1986).

[57] The tensions between these two viewpoints reflect various differences in Scripture. Thus, at the Creation, God gives man dominion over the animals but does not offer them to man for food: 'I have given you every herb bearing seed, which is upon the face of all the earth, and every tree, in the which is the fruit of a tree yielding seed; to you it shall be for meat' (Gen. 1:29). However, after the flood this is extended to include animals as well, when God says to Noah and his sons, 'Every moving thing that liveth shall be meat for you; even as the green herb have I given you all things' (Gen. 9:3).

Arguably, the same tension is reflected in the evangelists' differing versions of Our Lord's charge to his disciples, 'Go ye therefore, and teach all nations' (Matt. 28:19); 'Go ye into all the world, and preach the gospel to every creature' (Mark 16:15); 'repentance and remission of sins should be preached ... among all nations' (Luke 24:47).

[58] 'Take therefore no thought for the morrow: for the morrow shall take thought for the things of itself. Sufficient unto the day is the evil thereof' (Matt. 6:34).

awkwardly with conservation of the natural world for future generations, while if the universe itself is of intrinsic worth, respect for it by preservation of its resources is less to do with caring for the morrow than for recognising the value of the birds of the air and the grass of the field. Humankind's role becomes one of guardian, and like a faithful steward, the account of this guardianship should show that due increase which reveals our cooperation with God in the divine purpose of fruitfulness, reflected in Christ's parable of the talents.[59] In relation to the land, it signifies a respect for the productiveness and fruitfulness of a limited resource, which leads to its being exploited with due reverence for its being a divine gift, a due reverence that leads to a refusal to diminish, let alone exhaust, its productive capacity, but that would rather seek enhancement or increase. Sustainable growth would be the aim; non-exploitation would be as unacceptable as overexploitation in that it would be an abdication of humanity's God-given role within the created order.[60]

Even non-renewable resources, which by definition cannot be sustained, deserve to be exploited in order to achieve growth, always ensuring due respect for their being a divine gift. To refuse to exploit them would be to spurn the bounty of the divine giver; to exploit them irresponsibly would show a similar lack of respect. However, in relation to these resources, the Christian perspective differs from that of others concerned with environmental welfare in that it views responsible exploitation as a taking in faith, a faith that, although the resource will one day be exhausted, God will still provide. A Christian outlook refuses

---

[59] Matt. 25:14–30; Luke 19:11–27. See also A. Dunn in this volume, nn. 11–13.

[60] Sustainable *development* was defined by the Brundtland Commission as 'development which meets the needs of the present without compromising the ability of future generations to meet their own needs'; see World Commission on Environment and Development, *Our Common Future, Report of the Brundtland Commission* (Oxford, Oxford University Press, 1987), at 8. The European Union has since recognised the importance to the citizens of its member states that its policies should aim at patterns of development that respect the environment and are capable of being sustained over time. Its principle of sustainable *growth* has been built into article 2 of the Treaty of the European Community as amended by the Maastricht and Amsterdam Treaties. This is not to pretend that the terminology is free from difficulty; see, for instance, M. Redclift, *Sustainable Development: Exploring the Contradictions* (London, Methuen, 1987). The background and issues are well discussed in S. Elworthy and J. Holder, *Environmental Protection: Text and Materials* (London, Butterworth, 1997), 132–164. For an excellent discussion of the specifically Christian contribution to environmental law and the concept of sustainable development, see David Harte, 'A Christian Approach to Environmental Law?' in Beaumont, *Christian Perspectives on Law Reform*, 51–82.

to take thought for the morrow – in the sense of undue concern regarding the future – because it is rooted in the belief that a God who lovingly creates also lovingly sustains his creation,[61] and is aware that the history of God's provision has seen the discovery of new resources to replace the old, as for instance timber was replaced by fossil fuels, fossil fuels by oil, and as hydro, nuclear and now wind and solar energy have been brought into play to meet humankind's needs. With non-renewable as with renewable resources, a level of conservation that frustrated increase and improvement would be unacceptable, because it would be in contravention of the divine command to be fruitful and, as in the parable of the talents, to make use of what the Lord provides.[62]

That the law can supply models for such stewardship of land is fairly evident. Within the common law tradition, one can think of the standards of stewardship expected of a leasehold tenant in England and Wales, for instance, or the tenant for life under the Settled Land Acts.[63] Each had a duty not to commit waste. Thus activities or inactivity that led to the devaluation of the property for future owners were rendered unlawful under the various heads of waste recognised by common law and equity. Trustees likewise in their management and control of trust property are under various duties to balance the interests of current

---

[61] 'your Father knoweth that ye have need of these things' (Luke 12:30). Without such faith, hope for the future is reduced to what might be termed a Micawberish perspective – something will turn up, although there is no reason to believe that Dickens's character's optimism was not grounded on a simple but ultimately profound trust in the goodness of his Maker. See also Matt. 6:25–34.

[62] The Brundtland Commission believed that poverty was essentially evil, and that *widespread* poverty was no longer an inevitability. Indeed, sustainable development, as defined by the Commission, required meeting the basic needs of all and extending to all the opportunity to fulfil their aspirations for a better life. Poverty was a cause of ecological and other disasters. See World Commission on Environment and Development, *Our Common Future, Report of the Brundtland Commission*, at 8. That such growth – a growth without greed – provides the context for tackling problems of poverty, disease, ignorance and suffering is a powerful argument for recognising its role in the Christian task of preaching good news to the poor (cf. Matt. 11:4–5).

[63] Or at least until recently when strict settlements were prospectively abolished by the Trusts of Land and Appointment of Trustees Act 1996. No new strict settlements can now be created, but existing strict settlements continue. Lessees have been under a duty not to commit waste since the Statute of Marlborough 1267, and frequently are under a duty to keep the premises in good repair. Tenants for life have been subjected to trustee controls since the passing of the Settled Land Act 1882, s. 53; their duty is now set out in the Settled Land Act 1925, s. 107 (1).

beneficiaries against those with future interests. The rule in *Howe* v *Dartmouth*[64] provides an example. In civil law countries, the usufructuary likewise is under a duty to use and enjoy the property, subject to the usufruct, so as not to diminish its substance, *salve rerum substantia*, so that its productive capacity is entire at the end of the usufructuary's period of interest.[65] Whereas a usufructuary is not permitted to change the user of land and the common law tenant was once deemed guilty of causing ameliorating waste even if he changed the user for the better, such steps today are normally subject to obtaining permission from a statutory authority, that is, regulated by public rather than private law.[66] This gives rise to the question of how Christian ideas and ideals of stewardship can be successfully introduced into the workings of modern land management.

VII. How Can Stewardship be Ensured?

If the duty of the Christian can be summed up in the two great commandments of loving God and loving neighbour,[67] then in relation to the stewardship of property including land this requires that land be managed and exploited in a way that respects, indeed reveres, property as a gift from God and respects the interests and feelings of all others who are affected by one's actions and omissions in the management of that property.

In relation to the second of these duties, legal systems already do a great deal to ensure proper stewardship. Owners are today, and have generally in the past, been required to take into account the impact of their exercise of the powers of ownership upon their neighbours and future generations of their family with expectations of inheriting the property. Thus harmful activities are preventable and standards of conduct are imposed by the law upon owners. Moreover, as has been shown, even legitimate activities may be restrained if undertaken for bad motives rather than for the true benefit of the owner. As a result of the aggrandisement of the powers of owners implicit in the absolute conception of ownership at the start of the

---

[64] (1802) 7 Ves. 137.

[65] See, for instance, for France, *Code civil*, art. 578; for Spain, *Código civil*, art. 467; for Italy, *Codice civile*, art. 981.

[66] Thus converting dilapidated store buildings into dwellings, a farm into a market garden and a chapel into a cinema, have all been characterised as waste: see respectively, *Doherty* v *Allman* (1878) 3 App. Cas. 709; *Meux* v *Cobley* [1892] 2 Ch. 253; *Hyman* v *Rose* [1912] A.C. 623. For a discussion of the common law doctrine of waste, see (1950) 13 Conv. (N.S.) 278 (M.E. Bathurst). Today, planning permission for many such changes would be required under the Town and Country Planning Acts.

[67] Matt. 22:37–39.

nineteenth century, public law has also intervened to ensure that owners do not develop or run down their estates in such a manner as to damage the wider interests of the community or even today to impoverish the national or international heritage of all people.[68] In this, there is a shade of the Roman conception of some things being common to all people; a modern lawyer might categorise a legitimate interest, in the Italian sense, in the heritage of humankind as one such thing. Modern civil law systems also raise the interests of succeeding generations in property above those of the current owner as far as absolute control goes. A parent or other ancestor may not diminish his or her patrimony to defeat the legitimate expectations of their offspring. The birth of a child automatically invalidates an earlier will in most civil law countries and *inter vivos* gifts that have the effect of diminishing the portion of the estate reserved to the family in inheritance may be set aside or at least scaled down at the prejudiced person's request to ensure they get their due share as defined by law.[69]

It would therefore be fair to say that with regard to the family and neighbours the law not only can, but in many instances does, ensure a proper stewardship of property including land. It is worth reflecting that many of the regulatory devices that achieve this were developed during

---

[68] P. McAuslan, *Ideologies of Planning Law* (Frankin, Pergamon, 1980), states, 'The three competing ideologies are as follows: firstly, that the law exists and should be used to protect private property and its institutions; this may be called the traditional common law approach to the role of law. Secondly, the law exists and should be used to advance the public interest, if necessary against the interest of private property; this may be called the orthodox public administration and planning approach to the role of law. Thirdly, the law exists and should be used to advance the cause of public participation against both the orthodox public administration approach to the public interest and the common law approach to the overriding importance of private property; this may be called the radical or populist approach to the role of law' (at 3). In many respects, the history of public regulation of property over the last two centuries is the story of the re-emergence of the second factor and the recognition of the third. One can trace this in the development of planning legislation from the first Town and Country Planning Act in 1932 to its 1990 successor (in Scotland the progress from 1947 to 1972). There are also the initiatives taken and developed in the Clean Air Acts 1956 and 1968, the Environmental Protection Act 1990 and the Environment Act 1995, as well as very specific controls in relation to, for instance, tree preservation (Town and Country Planning Act 1990, s. 198) and listed buildings and conservation (Planning (Listed Buildings and Conservation Areas) Act 1990). The concept of heritage has become increasingly important in domestic, European and international law.

[69] For the history of this concept in civil law systems see Watkin, *Historical Introduction*, 192–218.

those centuries in which western legal systems were being developed in the context of a thoroughly Christianised society, although it must be admitted that some of the protective devices, having their roots in classical Roman law, predate the Christianisation of the western legal tradition. One should never however lose sight of the fact that even within the context of the modern, secular, pluralist state, a substantial number of constitutional rights and legal duties reflect the profound impact and inspiration of the Christian faith upon our legal as well as our general culture.

It is however more difficult to achieve a legal insurance of the fulfilment of the duty towards God regarding respect for the created order. This is largely the result of the vastly increased possibilities for exploitation of land that have resulted from the industrial and technological advances of the last few centuries, which advances have coincided, to our possible detriment, with the functional view of the world and absolute conceptions of ownership. As both of these latter factors have suffered decline, so there has developed an increased awareness, by no means confined to people with a perspective of faith, of the need to respect the earth and the environment, and not to harm the planet or our more local habitats by irresponsible exploitation. Numerous movements, from the local through the national to the international, have grown up ostensibly to restrain overexploitation and to protect both the interests of future generations and those of other living things, and indeed of the planet itself, reflecting the variations within the theology of stewardship that regard the moral community as consisting at least of humans, or even all animals or all living things, or even the entirety of creation.[70]

Again, despite the distinctly secular colour of many of these movements, the presence (albeit unconscious) of essentially Christian values within their thinking cannot be gainsaid. Indeed, it presents a missionary challenge to the Christian community not so much to inject Christian values into the teachings of those movements but to raise their awareness of that presence. The fact that such movements are significant players in

---

[70] These range from local conservation and amenity societies, through to national and international organisations. On the domestic scene, there has been the emergence since the 1970s of Green parties, of which *Die Grünen* in Germany has been particularly successful. In Germany a group called *Christen bei den Grünen* has worked closely with the Green Party. The World Wide Fund for Nature has also built bridges with Christian groups, as a result of an initiative taken by H.R.H. the Duke of Edinburgh, establishing a Network on Conservation and Religion. The World Wide Fund for Nature was responsible together with the United Nations Environment Programme and the World Conservation Union for the report *Caring for the Earth: A Strategy for Sustainable Living* (UNEP, Gland, 1991), which was a response in part to the Brundtland Report.

the national and international political arenas presents the Christian community with a better opportunity than has existed for several generations to seize the moment to underpin the importance of Christian values to society in the regulation of its stewardship of land and other forms of property. The collapse of alternative political schools that challenged the primacy of individual freedom in the control of property and the means of production, such as Soviet communism and several varieties of fascism, also enlarge the opportunities for the Christian community today.

If *Carpe Diem* is therefore the message of this part of the chapter, it is at least a day worth seizing. The signs of the times are auspicious for a strong Christian *putsch* in favour of subjecting our management of the creation as individuals, families, communities, nations and as an international community to a stern critique from a Christian perspective. Forces should be joined with the other interest groups engaged in this endeavour, to make them aware of the Christian dimension of their thought, a missionary goal, and to further the chances of political success in this objective, in much the same way as in earlier times the church allied itself with secular powers to further its goals.[71]

Indeed, one of the difficulties faced by those wishing to ensure proper stewardship of land from the perspective of due respect for the Creator's gifts is that within a democratic pluralist society the task is mountainous, given that each citizen has individual autonomy in relation to his or her own convictions on such issues. In past ages with a greater degree of hierarchy within society, such as during the Roman imperial period and during the centuries of feudalism and absolute monarchy, the task of Christian missionaries was in some ways easier, or at least the target plainer. Their task was to convert the ruler; the subjects would follow as a matter of course.[72] Although today, the right to attempt persuasion is more secure, the constituency that has to be converted is inestimably greater, and it would be a hard labour indeed to have to convert each owner to a Christian perspective in order to ensure proper stewardship. This is again why it is so important to join forces with likeminded interest groups to be able to achieve a clear, democratic majority for

---

[71] This would appear to be an apposite application of Our Lord's words 'he who is not against us is for us' (Luke 9:50). As Teresa Sutton has written, 'Christians need to be prepared to work with others including those who might be seeking similar ends but for completely different motives. That collaboration in itself is part of the spreading of the Gospel. Just as with other areas of Christian life, no easy route is guaranteed': see Teresa Sutton, 'Christians as Law Reformers in the Nineteenth and Twentieth Centuries', in Beaumont, *Christian Perspectives on Law Reform*, 7–24 at 24.

[72] The target would of course always have been to convert all, but the strategy would be simpler. Conversion of the ruler would lead with relative ease to the education of his people within the faith.

developing public law controls to ensure proper standards with regard to the exploitation and conservation of land as a given resource.[73]

The movement from preventing harm and protecting interests to seeking to ensure proper individual management is a difficult one. Of the Roman jurist Ulpian's three precepts of the law, *alterum non laedere* and *suum cuique tribuere* are easier to achieve than *honeste vivere*. How, it must be asked, can one through law make people virtuous. The answer undoubtedly is that one cannot, but one can create social structures that encourage goodness and avoid establishing institutions that discourage or even undermine Christian values in this as in other fields. Essentially, this is to encourage rather than enforce moral behaviour, and demands a renewed recognition that certain conduct, although lawful, remains wrong, and that the law should discourage and even condemn it without necessarily punishing those who perpetrate it.

One of the first problems with seeking to introduce standards of management applicable to all owners is that this would be perceived to be an interference with the freedom of owners in exercising their ownership, an attitude derived from the concept of ownership as absolute and a natural right, but nevertheless the one from which most modern thinking begins. It is therefore important to be able to put alongside this a distinct constitutional right to a sustainable environment in which to live. The inclusion of such as a fundamental right is important because it leaves the right to private property as one to be balanced against other legitimate interests.[74] However, given that one begins from a position in which owners believe that they have complete freedom to do as they wish with their own, any further restriction upon the limits of their freedom should be compensated.[75] French *droit administratif* has recognised this need and

---

[73] A powerful example of how scriptural authority can combine with modern juridical thinking is given by David Harte in discussing the precautionary principle; see David Harte, 'A Christian Approach to Environmental Law?' in Beaumont, *Christian Perspectives on Law Reform*, 51–82, at 71.

[74] It may be objected that the language of rights is inappropriate in this context, as to the Christian what needs to be recognised is a duty owed by humanity to God or to the created order itself to be a good steward. However, it can equally be argued that humanity's position within the created order as God's steward involves each human being having a duty to God to ensure that everyone respects the integrity of God's creation and that that necessarily requires that individuals be enabled to claim as of right that others, including governments and states, observe their duties in this regard. This means in turn that they require a right to claim that these others do their duty, and, for such a right to be good against governments, it needs to be a fundamental or constitutional right.

[75] See Article 1 of the First Protocol to the European Convention on Human Rights, which contains a requirement for compensation when government expropriates private property. The article is discussed in J.A. Frowein, 'The

acted upon it courageously.[76] There can be no excuse for not compensating owners for diminishing their powers; indeed, the difference could be between alienating them and obtaining their support. Thereafter, the taxation of profits from enterprises concerned in any way with the exploitation of land should reward good stewardship and penalise those owners who disregarded the required standards of guardianship. Having been compensated for any diminution of their freedom, there would hardly be cause for complaint. Moreover, the balance should be in the direction of encouragement. Past experience of attempting to compel owners to follow state standards suggests that compulsion is not as effective as encouragement; communist confiscation of the means of production was less effective in improving land management than Roman *emphyteusis*, the medieval leasing of lands in villeinage or even the *metayer* and *mezzadria* of more modern Mediterranean societies.[77]

Among the attitudes to be discouraged must be numbered greed and needless competition. The idea that the greater the increase in productivity and profit, the greater the success, needs to be replaced with structures that value growth as a sign of grace and respond with thankfulness.[78] A culture that expects no more than, and is thankful for, a just reward has to be created if proper stewardship is to be achieved as a

---

[75] (continued) Protection of Property', in R. St.J. Macdonald, F. Matscher and H. Petzold (eds.), *The European System for the Protection of Human Rights* (London, Nijhoff, 1993); L. Condorelli in L.-E. Pettiti, E. Decaux and P.-H. Imbert (eds.), *La Convention Européene des Droits de l'homme* (Paris, Economica, 1995).

[76] See, for instance, the decisions of the Conseil d'État in *La Fleurette* (CE 14 janvier 1938), *Compagnie Generale d'Energie Radioelectrique* (CE 30 mai 1966), and *Ministre des Affaires Etrangères c. Consorts Burgat* (CE 29 octobre 1976).

[77] For France, see *Code rural*, art. 937; for Spain, *Código civil*, art. 1628–1654; for Italy, *Codice civile*, art. 957–977.

[78] All forms of competition are not unhealthy, but some undoubtedly are. While competition can encourage the development of excellence and fulfilment of potential, the question of what constitutes excellence and the fulfilment of potential cannot, it is submitted, be divorced from the needs of society at a given time. It appears perverse to encourage growth in the knowledge that this will lead to depletion of scarce or limited resources or damage to other social interests. For instance, should a wealthy corporation feel obligated by law to develop open space which it has acquired as successor in title to a public body against the wishes of local residents because its legal duty is to ensure maximum profits, rather than reasonable profits, for its shareholders? Similarly, is there anything to be gained from placing schools, hospitals or industrial concerns and businesses into league tables measuring their success if all are performing well? This is not to say that the best should not be rewarded, but should the acceptably good be placed at the risk of being thought poor by comparison merely because they are less good?

long-term goal. While reward must properly reflect achievement, a competitive outlook should be discouraged. It is not I think fanciful to see the narrative of Abel and Cain in Genesis as an early essay in the appalling consequences of an overcompetitive spirit. Ultimately, the Christian concepts of a just price and a just wage have to be reinvigorated if Christian standards of good stewardship of the creation are to be viable.

As these last comments demonstrate, stewardship of land is not separable as a subject from the regulation of commerce by Christian principle nor ultimately from the spiritual development of the persons who feature as the legal subjects of property relations. The growth of principles of good stewardship in relation to land would be a sign of a society progressing along Christian lines and of spiritual as well as material prosperity in the individuals of whom that society was composed. The management of land as a natural resource is one manifestation of humanity's respect for the created order over which the Creator has given a dominion meant to be exercised in his, the Creator's, image. To accept the challenge of that responsibility is ceasing to be seen as a matter of choice, ironically in our largely secular age, but is nevertheless a call to fulfil the spiritual destiny of the species to grow into the Christlike subjects of the kingdom of God which is the Christian's hope and inheritance.

VIII. Conclusion

It has been the purpose of this chapter to demonstrate that over the centuries law has been both useful and effective in limiting the tendencies of owners to do whatever they wish with their own regardless of the interests as opposed to the rights of others, and that the absolute concept of ownership taken by many to be the norm in modern western life is the creature in effect of the last two and a half centuries only. In other words, those who advocate limiting the powers of owners with regard to their property need feel no embarrassment born of a major departure from the legal culture of the west in this regard.

To ensure proper stewardship in a Christian sense, indeed in the sense that Christians share with other interest groups, requires more, and it is not so apparent that the law can always ensure proper stewardship according to these standards. In *Caring for the Earth: A Strategy for Sustainable Living*, the World Conservation Union, in partnership with the United Nations Environment Programme and the World Wide Fund for Nature, presented a response to the Brundtland Report, *Our Common Future*. The report outlined nine principles that needed to be adopted for sustainable living. Some of these were clearly capable of being furthered and possibly achieved through legal regulation, for instance, minimising the depletion of non-renewable resources, providing national frameworks for integrating development and conservation and improving the quality of human life. It is possible to see such goals being promoted by programmatic legal regulation. However, when it comes to principles such as changing personal attitudes and practices, the place of law is not so evident. Practices can be regulated, but hardly attitudes. Ultimately, one is back with the Roman jurist Ulpian's precepts of law, and while it is possible to prohibit harming others and enabling each to receive his or her due, how does one ensure that people live virtuously? Law here can seek to encourage, but cannot alone fulfil. Humans can become virtuous through grace only, and that is the commodity, an awareness of which, Christians bring into the arena of the stewardship debate. As always, humans cannot succeed in isolation from God. Human law is limited by human failing, but its purposes are attainable through God's grace. It is the mission of those who strive to follow the teaching and example of Christ to confront the limitations of the human with the transcendent spiritual power of the divine. The limits of law, like the limits of life, are not limits to him who came that we should have life in its fullness.[79]

---

[79] The author wishes to thank Professor Paul Beaumont and the anonymous referees for their comments on an earlier draft of this chapter, and those who asked questions and participated in the discussion on the paper at the London Conference in September 1999. The author alone is responsible for whatever errors or infelicities remain.